The Rolling Stones

Titles in the People in the News series include:

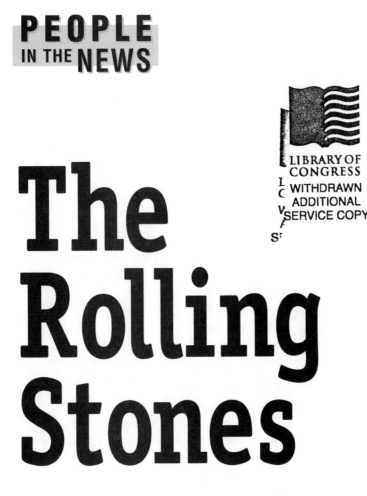

The
Rolling
Stones

by Stuart A. Kallen

Lucent Books, San Diego, CA

ML3930
.R64 K35
1999

Library of Congress Cataloging-in-Publication Data

Kallen, Stuart A., 1955–
    The Rolling Stones / by Stuart A. Kallen.
        p. cm. — (People in the news)
    Includes bibliographical references (p.   ).
    Summary: Traces the career of the English rock group that has been performing for over thirty-five years and is billed as "the world's greatest rock and roll band."
    ISBN 1-56006-435-8 (lib. : alk. paper)
    1. Rolling Stones—Juvenile literature. 2. Rock musicians—Biography—Juvenile literature. [1. Rolling Stones. 2. Musicians 3. Rock music.] I. Title. II. Series: People in the news (San Diego, Calif.)
ML3930.R64K35   1999
782.42166'092'2—dc21
[B]   98-35934
                                                                           CIP
                                                                       AC MN

Table of Contents

Foreword

FAME AND CELEBRITY are alluring. People are drawn to those who walk in fame's spotlight, whether they are known for great accomplishments or for notorious deeds. The lives of the famous pique public interest and attract attention, perhaps because their experiences seem in some ways so different from, yet in other ways so similar to, our own.

Newspapers, magazines, and television regularly capitalize on this fascination with celebrity by running profiles of famous people. For example, television programs such as *Entertainment Tonight* devote all of their programming to stories about entertainment and entertainers. Magazines such as *People* fill their pages with stories of the private lives of famous people. Even newspapers, newsmagazines, and television news frequently delve into the lives of well-known personalities. Despite the number of articles and programs, few provide more than a superficial glimpse at their subjects.

Lucent's People in the News series offers young readers a deeper look into the lives of today's newsmakers, the influences that have shaped them, and the impact they have had in their fields of endeavor and on other people's lives. The subjects of the series hail from many disciplines and walks of life. They include authors, musicians, athletes, political leaders, entertainers, entrepreneurs, and others who have made a mark on modern life and who, in many cases, will continue to do so for years to come.

These biographies are more than factual chronicles. Each book emphasizes the contributions, accomplishments, or deeds that have brought fame or notoriety to the individual and shows how that person has influenced modern life. Authors portray their subjects in a realistic, unsentimental light. For example, Bill Gates—the cofounder and chief executive officer of the software giant Microsoft—has been instrumental in making personal computers the most vital tool of the modern age. Few dispute his business savvy, his perseverance, or his technical expertise, yet critics say he is ruthless in his dealings with competitors and driven more by his desire to maintain Microsoft's dominance in the computer industry than by an interest in furthering technology.

In these books, young readers will encounter inspiring stories about real people who achieved success despite enormous obstacles. Oprah Winfrey—the most powerful, most watched, and wealthiest woman on television today—spent the first six years of her life in the care of her grandparents while her unwed mother sought work and a better life elsewhere. Her adolescence was colored by promiscuity, pregnancy at age fourteen, rape, and sexual abuse.

Each author documents and supports his or her work with an array of primary and secondary source quotations taken from diaries, letters, speeches, and interviews. All quotes are footnoted to show readers exactly how and where biographers derive their information and provide guidance for further research. The quotations enliven the text by giving readers eyewitness views of the life and accomplishments of each person covered in the People in the News series.

In addition, each book in the series includes photographs, annotated bibliographies, timelines, and comprehensive indexes. For both the casual reader and the student researcher, the People in the News series offers insight into the lives of today's newsmakers—people who shape the way we live, work, and play in the modern age.

Introduction

Ladies and Gentlemen, the Rolling Stones!

BY ALMOST ANY gauge used to measure rock and roll success, the Rolling Stones come out on top. They have been together longer, they have sold more records, they have played more concerts attended by more people, and they have made more money than any band in history.

Where Did They Come From?

The oldest Rolling Stone, Bill Wyman, was born William George Perks on October 24, 1936, in a tough neighborhood in southeast London. (After he joined the Stones, he took the modified last name of an army buddy, Lee Whyman, as his stage name.) Wyman's father was often unemployed and his youth was scarred by poverty. Food was scarce and the family's six children lived without luxuries. Wyman later said that everyone in the family used the same toothbrush, and each person had just one pair of socks, which was worn every day and laundered once a week.

Charles "Charlie" Robert Watts, the Stones' drummer, was born in London on June 2, 1941. His father was a truck driver and his mother was a housewife. From the time Watts was born until he reached age three, World War II was raging and warplanes from Nazi Germany were regularly dropping bombs on London. "I still can hear the bombs exploding in our neighbourhood," he later said. "I remember the mad rush from the house into the air-raid shelters."[1] Watts played banjo and rapped out tunes on his kitchen table with a knife and fork.

Lewis Brian Hopkins-Jones, or Brian Jones, the Stones' first rhythm guitarist, who also wrote the music for some of the band's best-known songs, was born in Gloucestershire, England, on February 28, 1942. Brian's father was an aeronautical engineer and his mother taught piano. Although Jones was taught to play classical piano by his mother, he soon became fascinated with jazz, a form of music his father would not tolerate in his house. As a result Jones became a rebel. He was often in trouble for dress-code violations, for drinking ale, and for skipping classes. Jones left the band in 1969 and died soon after.

Michael "Mick" Philip Jagger was born in Kent, England, on July 26, 1943. As a boy Mick had little interest in music. His father was a physical education teacher and his mother was a hairdresser. The family did not own a record player, and there was not much music around the house. According to Mick's brother Chris, "My memory of Mick is how much time he spent studying, always with his books. I really think he wanted to be a businessman. I think Mick's main ambition as a boy was to be rich. Money meant a lot to him."[2]

Both born in Kent, England, Mick Jagger (right) and Keith Richards became the Rolling Stones' powerhouse songwriting team.

Keith Richards was also born in Kent, on December 18, 1943. Keith's father was wounded in World War II and worked for General Electric his entire life. His mother sold washing machines and played the ukulele. As an adolescent, Keith was a soloist in the Westminster Abbey choir, an event he recalls with amusement: "The weirdest part of it was that me and the other two guys who were the soloists, we were the three biggest hoods in the school, and there we were singing like angels down at Westminster Abbey at Christmas, with our tight jeans underneath the surplices [choir robes]."[3]

The sixth, and often unrecognized Stone, pianist Ian Stewart, was born in the fishing village of Fife, Scotland, on July 18, 1939. Stewart, known as Stu, was "demoted" by band manager Andrew Loog Oldham before the first Stones abum was released. Oldham felt that Stu's looks were too rough, unpolished, and "common," and they did not mesh with the image the band was trying to project.

Although Stu did not appear in group photographs or get listed in band personnel information, he continued to play on records and in concert with the Stones and basically helped Jones start the band. Years later, when asked about being fired, Stu replied, "I had nothing better to do at the time, so I figured I would stay with them anyway, and travel."[4] He became both a silent partner and a road manager who, besides playing piano, used his van to take the band to and from gigs in the early days. Stewart was the second founding member of the Stones. Ian Stewart died on December 12, 1985.

Guitarist Michael "Mick" Kevin Taylor was born January 17, 1949, in Hertfordshire, England. Taylor joined the band in 1969, after the death of Brian Jones, and remained until late 1974. Taylor was replaced by Ron Wood, who was born on June 1, 1947, in London.

What Have They Offered?

The Rolling Stones introduced teenagers to the African American, urban blues of Muddy Waters, Howlin' Wolf, Bo Diddley, and others. In fact, the Rolling Stones took their name from a

Since their first album debuted in 1964, fans have continued to nominate the Rolling Stones "the world's greatest rock and roll band."

Muddy Waters song. The band also played hits from black artists on the Motown label, and it was greatly influenced by the poetry and rock and roll music of Chuck Berry.

By the early 1970s the Stones had transformed the urban blues into a steady string of high-energy rock and roll hits such as "(I Can't Get No) Satisfaction," "Gimme Shelter," "Jumpin' Jack Flash," and "Brown Sugar." To their fans, they were the greatest rock and roll band in the world.

As children of the sixties, the Stones exuded the peace and love euphoria of the times, but their songs often referred to drugs, sex—and occasionally—the devil. So the Rolling Stones became the scapegoats for the hippie social revolution that was spearheaded—at least in part—by their music. The press and others reviled the Stones as an evil influence on teenagers.

This made the Stones notorious. There were violent riots at many of their concerts. In addition, band members and their wives or girlfriends were often arrested with a wide array of drugs. And drugs soon took their toll on the band. By the late seventies the Rolling Stones were ravaged by a "whirlpool of deaths, drug overdoses and wrecked lives."[5]

In the late 1980s, the five men who then made up the Rolling Stones got their act together and took to the stage stronger than ever. Millions of Americans bought tickets to see them. Their 1989 North American Steel Wheels tour set a world record for the most successful concert in history, earning $310

The Mother of Rock and Roll

Bluesman Muddy Waters said, "The blues had a baby, and they called it rock and roll." In his book *The Rolling Stones*, Robert Palmer writes about blues musician Robert Johnson, who inspired early blues players like Muddy Waters as well as the Rolling Stones, Jimi Hendrix, Eric Clapton, and others.

> Robert Johnson, the black Delta blues singer who died in 1938 after drinking poisoned whiskey, was an evil genius, Lucifer's right-hand man. At least that's what the God-fearing . . . folk of rural Mississippi thought. Even young Muddy Waters, growing up in the Delta in the Thirties, believed the stories after he heard Johnson wailing "Hellhound on My Trail.". . . One afternoon when Muddy was in his teens, he spotted the legendary Robert Johnson singing and playing guitar on a small-town street corner. But Muddy was afraid to get a close look, "because," he explained years later, "people said the Devil taught Robert Johnson to play the blues. They said he was a dangerous man."

> The blues acquired its sinister reputation because the people who played and listened to it were outcasts. . . . They were people who shunned preachers as hypocrites . . . preferring to put their faith in the conjure men and root doctors who were keeping the old African religions alive. . . . The blues people began to wonder: What *is* evil, anyway? Is it nothing more than the reverse image . . . of good? And if good means the hypocritical values of the proper folk . . . and all the rest of the . . . baggage handed down by the [former] slave masters—if *that's* all good is . . . then evil just might be worth investigating. Several decades later, the Rolling Stones would come to similar conclusions.

million in thirty cities and playing to 3.2 million people. In 1997 the Rolling Stones' Voodoo Lounge tour sold more than 1.5 million concert tickets and grossed more than $89 million.

Fans continued to nominate the Rolling Stones as "the world's greatest rock 'n' roll band," a title bassist Bill Wyman says "we never claimed, but never denied."[6] The Voodoo Lounge tour proved that the Stones were still commanding audiences three decades after their inception. And though it may be "only rock and roll," the fans still loved it.

Chapter 1

The Early Days

IN THE 1960s the Rolling Stones were constantly criticized by the press. They were called subversive, decadent, dirty, and a bad influence on the young. Author A. E. Hotchner suggests that their rebellious behavior might be understood as a reaction against the prospect of having to spend their lives in the bland, boring English suburbs.

> Perhaps it was the mounting pressure of wanting to escape these deadly towns that motivated young people to turn to one of the few avenues that afforded them a way out—music. Otherwise they were trapped in a system that apprenticed teenagers to the work their fathers performed—generations of tradition dictated that a bricklayer's son became a bricklayer, a railway worker's son went to work for the railway.[7]

Like many English children during the 1950s, Mick Jagger, Keith Richards, and Brian Jones were conformists. Mick and Brian were good students whose middle-class families afforded them opportunities. Keith's family was poor, but Keith was bright and creative. When Mick, Keith, and Brian reached the age of thirteen, however, they became rebels, using music as a catalyst for their rebellion. The music of Muddy Waters and Chuck Berry proved an easy escape from the stodgy mores of the English middle-class.

Jagger Meets Richards

Mick Jagger first met Keith Richards when both the boys were eight years old. Mick Jagger recalled:

Brian Jones, shown in a 1967 photo, was a rebellious teenager who openly defied his parents by listening to jazz music. The founding member of the band, Jones was the Stones' rhythm guitarist until 1969.

Keith and I went to school together . . . when we were about seven. We lived in the same block. We weren't great friends, but we knew each other. We also knew each other when we left school. I went to grammar school while Keith went to another school in the same village, so I used to see him riding to school on his bike.[8]

The two friends lost touch at age ten, when Richards moved to a tough neighborhood.

Richards later went to art college. In those days, art college drew many students who were more interested in folk or pop music than in art. He learned graphic arts and drawing while focusing on musical sessions held in empty classrooms. (Other alumni of England's art schools include David Bowie and members of the Who, the Beatles, the Yardbirds, and the Kinks.)

As the sixties dawned the art-school rockers were part of the first generation of young Englishmen who were not called up for compulsory military service. According to fashion designer Ossie Clark, "Everybody let their hair grow long as sort of a rebellious celebration at not having to have an army haircut. And the new clothes—all that outlandish getup—was a kind of rebellion against those years of necktie conformity."[9]

But while many British teenagers were trying to master homemade guitars and drum kits or were standing in front of mirrors practicing the moves of rock superstar Elvis Presley, Mick Jagger stood apart. As he recalls in an interview with author A. E. Hotchner:

> When I was thirteen the first person I really admired was Little Richard. I wasn't particularly fond of Elvis or Bill Haley—they were very good, but for some reason they didn't appeal to me. I was more into Jerry Lee Lewis, Chuck Berry and, a bit later, Buddy Holly.[10]

Jagger and Richards were also listening to musicians who were not well known in England: Bo Diddley, Muddy Waters, and Little Walter. Records by black blues artists were hard to find in Jagger's hometown, so the industrious teen sent a direct order to Chess Records in Chicago. Jagger was carrying some of those

Skiffle Music

The Rolling Stones, the Beatles, and many other English rock bands began as skiffle groups, which featured nonstandard instruments. The skiffle style was very popular in 1950s England. Harold Pendleton, owner of London's Marquee Club, talks about a friend's skiffle band in A. E. Hotchner's *Blown Away*.

> This little band was composed of a crude guitar, a homemade bass, a suitcase that was played on with whisk brooms, and a washboard strummed with thimbles. Chris [Barber] called it his skiffle group. He got the name from having read about the rent parties that used to be given in poor, Negro quarters to raise rent money—the blacks of New Orleans called them skiffle parties. . . . None of those poor [people] owned any real instruments, so the instruments of those skiffle bands had to be kazoos, papers and combs, whisk brooms on suitcases, dustbin [garbage can] basses, homemade guitars with strings on a board—like that. That's how the skiffle group came to be invented in England, and it caught on like wildfire. Skiffle bands sprung up everywhere because the kids didn't have to learn to play difficult instruments.

Skiffle was so popular that washboard factories had to work overtime to provide rhythm instruments for budding musicians.

Mick Jagger (pictured) was inspired by such artists as Chuck Berry, Bo Diddley, and Muddy Waters. Their music had a great influence on the sound of the Rolling Stones, whose own name was taken from a Muddy Waters song.

blues records when he ran into Richards one day in October 1961.

Jagger was at the train station in Dartford, Kent, on his way to classes at the prestigious London School of Economics. Richards was on his way to art college. Richards had recently taken up the guitar and could even imitate Chuck Berry's guitar licks. Jagger's armful of Muddy Waters albums piqued Richards's interest, and the guitarist invited his childhood acquaintance for a visit that afternoon. Richards's biographer, Victor Bockris, lets his subject tell what happened:

> "[Jagger] started playing a few records here and there," Keith recalled, "but when I eventually got to hear Muddy Waters, it all fell into place for me. He was the thing I was looking for, the thing that pulled it all in for me. When I heard him I realized the connection between all the music I'd heard. He made it all explainable. He was like a codebook. I was incredibly inspired by him as a musician. He was more than a guitar player, more than a singer, more than a writer. It was all him. He was the hoochie-coochie man." [11]

At the time, Jagger was playing in a band called Little Boy Blue and the Blue Boys. A month after their meeting, Richards joined Jagger's band.

The Licks of Brian Jones

Meanwhile, Brian Jones, who had become proficient at saxophone and guitar, was spending his time in coffee houses and jazz clubs near his home in western England. Jones was hooked on the music of slide-guitarist Elmore James, a Mississippi Delta bluesman. By early 1962 Jones had moved to London to be closer to the music scene.

The Ealing Club was the only jazz club in London that allowed electric guitars. Alex Korner and his band, Blues Incorporated (or Blues Inc.), played there. Jones was allowed to sit in with the band and he quickly gained notoriety performing the slide technique used by Elmore James. The slide guitar was virtually unknown at that time in England. Jones became a regular in Blues Incorporated, playing guitar and harmonica.

Alex Korner

In 1962, at the age of thirty-three, Alex Korner was the godfather of English blues. He ran the Ealing Club in a dirty, damp basement and started England's first electric rhythm and blues (R&B) band, Blues Incorporated, featuring future Stones drummer Charlie Watts. Blues music was basically unheard-of in England in the early sixties, and traditional jazz musicians resisted its introduction.

It was Korner's habit to let anyone who had the courage sit in with his band. He not only loved playing R&B himself but, as James Karnbach and Carol Bernson write in *It's Only Rock 'n' Roll,*

> [Korner] was a great supporter of other musicians, young and old, black and white, English and foreign. Traveling players always knew they would have a place to sleep in London—on Korner's kitchen floor. Blues Inc. itself nurtured the early careers of many now-famous musicians.

The Ealing was packed every night with musicians such as Eric Clapton, Eric Burdon, Jack Bruce, Ginger Baker, Paul Jones, Ron Wood, David Davies, and Jeff Beck to name a few. They would go on to form, among other groups, the Yardbirds, the Kinks, the Animals, Manfred Mann, Cream, the Faces, and Led Zeppelin.

Brian Jones decided it was time to form his own band, so he ran an ad in *Jazz News*. Pianist Ian Stewart was one of the first to answer the ad. Jagger and Richards later showed up at the audition together. Stewart's impressions of the new band were captured in an interview by A. E. Hotchner:

> I'd seen Brian perform, and I had been impressed with how much self-assurance he had when he played. He knew how to arouse the audience, doing many of the little sexy things that Jagger picked up and ran with later on. Richards and Jagger also had performed a few times at the Ealing—of course, all of it for nothing more than a free beer—but I didn't think either of them was anything to write home about. Mick sang off-key and was rather self-conscious, but he had enough of his raw moves to get a good reaction from the audience. Keith was stiff but had a good grasp of his guitar.
>
> But to tell the truth, I sure as hell wasn't impressed with these guys. It was obvious that Brian was a flake from the things he said, Mick and Keith looked like a couple of . . . panhandlers, both skinny and undernourished, Keith with his red nose and pimples, Mick all bones and always talking about food, which obviously was in short supply. In fact, they looked like they were both going to starve to death. Neither had a shilling to his name—all Mick had to live on was a seven-pounds-a-week student grant, and Keith was totally dependent on what he could cadge off his mother. The less said about their clothes the better—every day they wore the same stuff, which they probably slept in. . . .
>
> Brian arranged for us to have our first rehearsal . . . and he had a name for us: the Rolling Stones, which he had copped from Muddy Waters's song, "Rollin' Stone Blues." I thought it was an awful name and I told Brian so. People would expect to see a group of Irish acrobats, I told him. The others didn't seem to care one way or another. Of course, a name's not important until you start to get booked—and we were a long, long way from that.[12]

First Gigs as the Rolling Stones

Soon Jagger, Richards, and Jones were roommates. They lived in a grungy apartment with peeling wallpaper, chairs with broken springs, a seldom-used coin-operated heater, and a single lightbulb hanging from the ceiling. Amidst the overflowing ashtrays and dirty dishes, the boys rehearsed constantly.

On July 11, 1962, the band played their first gig as the Rolling Stones, working through a set of rhythm and blues songs at a club called the Marquee. In September the band recorded three songs for a demo tape. Bill Wyman heard the band for the first time in early December, and the next week he auditioned for the job of bass player.

Wyman had worked with several rock groups and held a day job to support his wife and child. He had plenty of experience and had been playing regular gigs in London. By all accounts, his "monster amp" and other equipment are what got him into the band. Richards's biographer presents these recollections:

> "They didn't like me," Wyman said. "But I had a good amplifier, and they were badly in need of amplifiers at that time! So they kept me on."

> "He was a real London Ernie," Richards said. "Brylcreemed hair and eleven-inch cuffs on his pant and huge blue suede shoes with rubber soles."[13]

Although Wyman played gigs with the band, they continued to advertise for another bass player.

The Stones had jammed with Charlie Watts a few times at the Ealing, but they could not afford to have him in the band. The drummer himself tells why:

> They were working a lot of dates without getting paid. . . . And there was me earning a pretty comfortable living, which was obviously going to nosedive if I got involved in the Rolling Stones. But . . . I liked their spirit. . . . So I said, OK, yes, I'd join. Lots of my friends thought I'd gone raving mad.[14]

Before joining the Stones, Brian Jones (left) became well known in London for imitating the unusual techniques of slide-guitarist Elmore James. In this 1966 photo, Jones performs with Mick Jagger.

Watts, who played his first gig with the Stones on January 17, 1963, kept his day job as a graphic artist at an advertising agency. Before long, however, the band would become a full-time position for the fledgling graphic artist.

Playing the Clubs

The year 1963 proved a turning point for the Rolling Stones. In February the band was hired to play at the Crawdaddy Club after a previously scheduled act canceled. This turned into a regular Sunday night gig for the Stones. The owner of the Crawdaddy, Giorgio Gomelsky, soon joined up as the band's manager.

At first the Stones played blues and rock while sitting on stools, and they attracted a quiet, polite audience. "But," according to rock historian and critic Robert Palmer, "they didn't remain seated for very long, and neither did the student and artsy dropout types who came to hear them." [15] Everyone began shaking. Jagger shook tambourines and maracas. Jones shook his mop of long blond hair. Fans stood on tables and chairs,

Inspired by the Blues

While others may debate the importance of the 1960s and the rock and roll bands of that decade, Bill Wyman, who was there, has a unique perspective on those times and the times that followed. His book, *Stone Alone,* contains this analysis:

Pop music was never meant to endure, but the best of the rock 'n' roll born in the sixties survives well. There are two main reasons. First, we young musicians were mining gold, the rich source of our inspiration being black or black-inspired music. That wellspring of our fervor seemed lost on the generation of rock bands that succeeded us. To them, we were the Establishment, and they took their cue from us with little knowledge of our heritage. They had superior technology, but their sources were second-hand. Secondly, bands like ours blossomed alongside important social change. Battles were fought and won in the sixties. The fifties, when the Stones were teenagers, had been grey years in Britain, when we paid the price of wartime and we had no real voice. By the start of the sixties, we were ready to assert ourselves forcefully: long hair became OK; an anti-Establishment attitude among teenagers suited the Stones perfectly; experimentation with drugs became prevalent, if controversial, entering the lives of many rock musicians; and with the permissive society came the arrival of the birth-control pill.

For these years of revolution, the Stones helped provide the soundtrack. They were heady and combative times, when the sun shone on us and we carried a torch for individuality against conservatism.

Bill Wyman remained the Stones' bass player for thirty years, despite the band's early misgivings about having him in the band.

The Stones' energetic and engaging performances quickly drew large, enthusiastic crowds.

shaking to the pulsating rhythms. The Stones' sets became sweaty, exhausting, and curiously elating. Palmer describes the band during this period:

> Brian and Mick, the band's most outgoing performers, were otherwise very different. Brian played to the girls in the audience, nailing the prettiest ones with eye contact. Mick was still shy, but he had those strange, big, pouty lips, and when he shook his thin hips, some of the girls thought he was sexier than Brian. Keith, who stood off to one side playing his guitar, already had the raffish look of a highwayman. Bill, dark and saturnine [sullen], older than the others and a family man, seemed utterly disdainful of everything but the bass lines with which he firmly anchored the music. Charlie drummed away, looking tough and enigmatic. They were disparate personalities, these five, but already they had a chemistry, a special balance, a group identity.[16]

Chapter 2

Up and Down in Rock and Roll

WITHIN SIX WEEKS, the Stones' audience at the Crawdaddy had grown from a handful of people to three hundred rowdy, screaming fans. At the time, British rock critic Nik Cohen described the sound of the Stones:

> They lay down something very violent in the lines of rhythm and blues. They were enthusiasts then; they cared a lot about their music. . . . They were mean and nasty, full blooded, very testy, and they beat out the toughest, crudest, most offensive noise an English band had ever made. . . . Naughty but nice, they were liked by the . . . hitch-hikers, beards and freaks and pre-Neanderthal Mods everywhere. Simply, they were turning into the voice of hooliganism. . . . Keith Richards wore T-shirts. All the time, he kept winding and unwinding his legs, ugly like a crab; he was shut in, shuffling, the classic school drop-out.[17]

The band was dedicated to the blues, and they learned everything they could about that musical style. They also knew that they would find freedom in that knowledge—the freedom to play their own blues—but all of them, especially Jagger, were determined to achieve commercial success.

On April 21, 1963, Andrew Loog Oldham stopped by the Crawdaddy to watch the Stones. Oldham was a well-connected nineteen-year-old publicist who handled press for the Beatles. The Beatles were on their way to becoming the biggest pop sensation

Andrew Oldham predicted that the Stones would be superstars the first time he saw them perform and signed the band to a three-year management contract.

in years. "Beatlemania" was about to sweep across the globe and the "Fab Four," as they were known, were destined to become the most popular rock group of the decade.

As Keith Richards says, the Stones were trying to be the anti-Beatles:

> It was the beginnings of Beatlemania. . . . They've got a harmonica. We'd heard they did Chuck Berry songs, but being a pop star did not even come into the realm of possibilities [for the Stones]. We saw no connection between us and the Beatles; we were playing the blues, they were singing pop songs dressed in suits. They were an encouraging sign in a new trend in popular music, but to be in the charts, or to be pop stars—we were almost a reaction against that. We were not hip to be pop stars, it was like the only dignity we had left.[18]

Oldham insisted from the first time he heard the Stones that they would be a huge commercial success. Before the week was out, he had signed the Stones to an exclusive three-year management contract, giving the five Stones a 6 percent share. (Ian Stewart was kept on as a road manager and paid a nominal salary.)

Into the Studios

A week after signing with Oldham, the Stones were in London's Olympic Studio recording Chuck Berry's "Come On," their first single for Decca Records. Oldham had never produced a record before; as a result, the Stones' first single was recorded in a rush and was badly mixed. Fans did not seem to care, though. After its release in June, "Come On" climbed to number twenty-one on the British charts. The Rolling Stones were on their way.

In July, the band went into the ITV television studios to make their TV debut on the pop music program *Thank Your Lucky Stars*. They reluctantly appeared in identical outfits— velvet-collared houndstooth check jackets, complete with coordinated ties and pants. In August the Stones appeared on another pop music show called *Ready, Steady, Go!*

By the time the Stones came onto the rock scene, the Beatles (pictured) were already a huge sensation. The Stones, however, tried hard to be unlike the Beatles in everything from musical style to dress.

In September 1963 the Rolling Stones began their first tour of the United Kingdom. They were the opening act for the Everly Brothers and Bo Diddley. Little Richard joined the bill later in October. As 1963 drew to a close, the Rolling Stones were well on their way to becoming the biggest rock group in England, second only to the Beatles. Second-place status did not seem to bother them, however. In fact, their second single was "I Wanna Be Your Man," written by John Lennon and Paul McCartney of the Beatles. The single was backed by a song called "Stoned." This song, written by the entire band, was credited to "Nanker Phelge." ("Nanker" was the nickname for an unpleasant facial expression band members made, and "Phelge" was the surname of an early roommate of Richards, Jagger, and Jones, whose personal hygiene left something to be desired.)

Life changed for the Rolling Stones after the release of their first single. No longer an unknown blues group crowded into a filthy apartment, they became concert, television, and recording

Following the 1963 release of their first single, a cover of Chuck Berry's "Come On," the Stones became well-known concert, television, and recording stars.

stars. Still, the life of a rock idol is by no means a vacation. The band was living in cheap hotels and tour buses and were still only paid £20 to £60 per show. (These amounts, in British pounds, are equivalent to about $40 to $120 at today's exchange rates). Brian Jones, an asthmatic all his life, missed dozens of gigs because of various illnesses.

Frenzied Fans

Rock and roll bands had instigated rowdy behavior—and even riots—in audiences since the mid-1950s. By the early 1960s millions of post–World War II baby boomers were entering into their boisterous teenage years. And the energy of white rhythm and blues (R&B) as played by the Stones, struck a chord with teenage girls in particular. The Stones had played to raving audiences before, but as they became more popular, the frenzy of the fans increased. As Bill Wyman writes,

> the gig I shall always remember from this time was the one we played at Lowestoft, Suffolk on 6 September 1963. This was our first experience of teenage girls rushing the stage wanting our bodies. We stayed in great rooms at the Grand Hotel, where the show took place before 1,200 people. Halfway through the performance, girls attacked us on stage, tearing off our clothes. I thought to myself: 'Well, there's nothing I can do. I must keep playing.' I had half my shirt ripped away and buttons torn from my leather waistcoat. It happened to all four of us (Brian was out sick at the time). We were paid £20 plus free accommodation.[19]

Richards tried to explain the behavior of the audience: "Maybe it had to do with World War II or some other social or political thing, but teenage girls needed that sort of frenzy. It was like a mating thing."[20]

The band crisscrossed England on two-lane roads, sleeping in the back of Ian Stewart's Volkswagen van. In the years before Britain's motorway (freeway) system was built, the band would play a gig, then spend all night driving to the next show. There was often little time to stop for food. But the band became

Keith Richards and Drugs

The history of Keith Richards's drug abuse has been covered in detail by the media. His long-running battle with heroin addiction has almost caused the Rolling Stones to break up dozens of times. In Victor Bockris's biography *Keith Richards*, the guitarist tells how he started using drugs.

> Usually drug taking in music starts off on a very, very mundane level—just keep going to make the next gig. They're nothing I'd recommend to anybody, drugs, but it's a musician's life—it's very difficult to get anyone to understand. It's an underworld life, anyway. Musicians start to work when everybody else stops working and wants some entertainment. If you get enough work, you're working three hundred fifty days a year because you want to fill up every gig. And you reach a point very early on when you're sitting around in the dressing room with some other acts in the show and you say, "I've gotta drive five hundred miles and do two shows tomorrow and I can't make it." And so you look around at the other guys and say, "How the hell have you been making it for all these years!" And they say, "Well, baby, take one of these." Musicians don't start off thinking, "We're rich and famous, let's get high." It's a matter of making the next gig.

Keith Richards's heavy drug use and heroin addiction nearly caused the band's demise on many occasions.

tighter and more integrated as they were thrown into hotel rooms together, shared stages and dressing rooms, ate, drank, and experienced the hysteria of their growing army of fans.

Knocking the Beatles off the Charts

The year 1964 started with great promise for the Rolling Stones. On January 2, 1964, the band appeared on the premiere broadcast of BBC-TV's *Top of the Pops,* performing "I Wanna Be Your Man." Four days later they began their first U.K. tour as headliners. On May 2 Decca released their first LP (long-playing vinyl album), simply titled *The Rolling Stones.* The cover was a darkly lit photo of the band with no name or title written on it. The music was an eclectic mix of electric blues (Slim Harpo's "King Bee" and Willie Dixon's "I Just Want to Make Love to You"); fifties rock ("Route 66" and Chuck Berry's "Carol"); and Motown soul ("Can I Get a Witness"). Although critics liked the album, Mick Jagger criticized the band's early recordings in a 1968 interview: "You could say we did the blues to turn people on, but why they should be turned on by us is unbelievably stupid. I mean, what's the point of listening to us doing 'I'm a King Bee' when you can hear Slim Harpo doing it?" [21]

The album resembles a typical set list of the live Stones performances of this period. The songs were recorded as if the band were playing them on stage. The album was a smash success. It knocked the Beatles off the top of the U.K. charts and sold a then-phenomenal one hundred thousand copies. (By 1997 the Stones had released thirty-six albums and five singles that sold over a million copies each, a world record.)

Meanwhile, the band had released its first single in the United States—a cover of the Bo Diddley song "Not Fade Away," backed by "I Wanna Be Your Man." In June the Stones released "It's All Over Now." Rock critic Robert Palmer was very impressed with the single:

> On "It's All Over Now" the Stones' awesome twin-guitar [Brian's and Keith's] firepower is plainly felt, and Keith unleashes the first of the great power-chord riffs with which he was about to revolutionize rock rhythms. . . .

Like a Battle Scene

As the Rolling Stones became more popular in 1964, their concerts
became riots. This madness is described in Victor Bockris's biography
Keith Richards.

> WYMAN: "We used to play three bars of the first song before the
> whole place fell to bits and they poured on stage and broke all
> the guitars. Every single day over a period of six months—every
> day a riot."
>
> RICHARDS: "It was like [a battle] going on, people gasping . . .
> chicks choking, nurses running around with ambulances. You
> took your life in your hands just to walk out there. I was stran-
> gled twice. It was like a living *Hard Day's Night* [the film in
> which the Beatles play themselves at the height of Beatlema-
> nia]—climbing over rooftops . . . getaways down fire escapes,
> through laundry chutes, into bakery vans. It was all mad."

Images of the Stones' concerts . . . were telegraphed in word bites like
"Ambulance men carried out hysterical teenager girls in strait-
jackets. . . . The performance was stopped in ten minutes because of
rioting teenagers. . . . Three thousand fans rioted as the Stones flew
in."

"I need an army to protect me," said Richards, who was almost
crushed to death, strangled, knocked unconscious, or electrocuted on
at least six occasions.

*A policeman is knocked to the ground by an unruly crowd trying frantically to
get closer to the band members during a 1966 Stones performance.*

Keith's backup singing . . . is a far cry from the Everlys' refined harmonies, but it does have a white country-music flavor. . . . It's no accident that it was also the first Stones single recorded in America at Chess studios in Chicago during the group's first American tour in 1964.[22]

Not Welcome in America

In May 1964 London Records released the band's first LP in the United States. Titled *The Rolling Stones—England's Newest Hitmakers,* the album included the song "Tell Me," the first Jagger/Richards composition to be recorded by the Stones (Gene Pitney had previously recorded a Jagger/Richards song, "That Girl Belongs to Yesterday").

On June 1 the Stones arrived in the United States for their first American tour. The next night they made their first U.S. television appearance on the *Les Crane Show,* a local New York late-night program.

Keith Richards was absolutely thrilled to be in America. As he later told his biographer, Victor Bockris,

> we thought, "This is the payoff!" We got to fly to America, just to get there! To cats like Charlie and me, America was fairyland. Nobody in our lives had a way of getting there, even once, just for a visit! Forget it, no way. To be paid to go there and play to Americans, we were shi——ing ourselves.
>
> Nobody realizes how America blew our minds. I can't even describe what America meant to us. How can you measure it! We were enthralled and turned on with the idea of being in America, fairyland do you know what I mean! Once I got to the Astor Hotel it became a blur that day because we just went berserk.[23]

In New York City the band was greeted by the usual madness. Their hotel was mobbed by thousands of fans (mostly teenage girls), with only four policemen to hold back the crowd. The girls screamed, waved signs, and tried to force their way onto the band's limousines.

The band began their first American tour on June 5, 1964, at the Swing Auditorium in San Bernardino, California. The Stones played eleven songs for an audience of four thousand who screamed and went wild, throwing jelly beans at the stage and waving banners that said "We Love the Stones." Girls bounded onto the stage and grabbed at the musicians as policemen tried to drag off the intruders. All in all, the concert was a great success.

The rest of the two-week tour, however, turned out to be less than a dream come true. The band was regularly humiliated and insulted. Some of their concerts were sparsely attended. When the band walked through airports they were taunted with calls of "Cut your hair" and "Where's your lipstick?"

On one occasion the police came backstage and made the band pour their drinks—both whisky and soda—down the toilet. When Richards refused, a cop pulled a gun on him. Amer-

Recording at Chess Records

The recording studios at Chess Records were the epicenter of the blues and rock that the Stones so loved. On their first American tour, the band recorded four songs at Chess. In *Stone Alone*, Bill Wyman describes the sessions.

We went to a recording session at 2120 South Michigan Avenue, home of the legendary Chess Studios. . . . The engineer was Ron Malo (who did the recording for most of our idols). . . . It was a milestone event for us to be in an American studio, recording on 4-track. We knew the sound we were getting live in clubs and concerts was not what came across on the records we had cut in England. People were not used to that kind of roughness; a really good, funky American feel was what we were after. When we recorded at Chess . . . Malo knew exactly what we wanted and got it almost immediately. We felt we were taking part in a little bit of history there. . . . During the session we were thrilled to be visited by blues guitarist Buddy Guy and songwriter Willie Dixon (who tried to sell us some of his songs).

One thing shocked the Stones: Fifty-year-old bluesman Muddy Waters, who was not selling many records at the time, was working as a roadie for the studio. Wyman said: "As kids we would have given our right arms to say hello to [him], and there's the great Muddy Waters helping carry my guitar into the studio. . . . It was unreal."

Mick Jagger is mobbed by screaming fans at a London airport as the Stones depart for the United States for their first American tour. Despite a successful start, the two-week tour was largely a disappointment.

ica still favored clean-cut teen idols like Frankie Avalon, and few men had long hair. In the Midwest, the Stones played in five-thousand-seat auditoriums, however, only a mere one hundred people came to see them.

When the band appeared on the TV show *Hollywood Palace,* they were the first rock group to do so. The show's stage manager observed the band's attire (street clothes) and concluded that the musicians were too poor to afford the tuxedos usually worn by the show's performers. The Stones were offered white cable-knit sweaters, white shirts, white pants, and white shoes. Needless to say, the band was not interested.

Yet despite the largely disappointing reception in the United States, when the Stones returned to London thousands of screaming fans were waiting for them at the airport—even though it was seven o'clock in the morning.

Chapter 3

Topping the Charts

Good news greeted the Rolling Stones when the band returned to England after its first U.S. tour. "It's All over Now," had become their first number one single in the United Kingdom.

On August 8 the band played their first gig on the European continent. The concert, in The Hague, Netherlands, was scheduled to last an hour. The fans went insane as soon as the show started, however, and the band ran offstage after only two songs. Police mercilessly clubbed the audience with batons and the historic concert hall was left a total shambles.

The rest of the European tour was much the same. "Everywhere the Stones went, they created pandemonium—riots, police dogs, arrests, tear gas, brawls—the uglier the concerts became, the more the Stones won the esteem of the hordes of teenagers to whom they had become the symbol of what the sixties stood for." [24] The worst scene was in Warsaw, Poland, where two thousand fans tried to force their way into the theater where the Stones were playing. Police repelled them with tear-gas grenades, water cannons, and flailing clubs.

The Stones returned to the United States in October 1964. Well-known television variety host Ed Sullivan booked the band on his program, which gave the Stones their largest ever audience in America. On October 28 the band headlined the star-studded TAMI (Teen Age Music International) Show in Santa Monica, California. They played on the same bill as Chuck Berry, James Brown, and many soul artists from the Motown label. The concert was filmed, and this was the band's first appearance in a feature-length movie.

The Rolling Stones perform during a 1966 appearance on The Ed Sullivan Show. *The Stones' first appearance on the show in 1964 gave the band its largest American audience ever, helping to propel their popularity in the United States.*

January 1965 found the Stones touring Ireland and Australia. At the end of the month, Decca released the Stones' second album, *Rolling Stones No. 2*. Most of the album was recorded in Chicago. Like the band's first LP, *Rolling Stones No. 2*, also consisted of cover songs by black artists and the quality was uneven. (Cover tunes are popular songs that a musician "covers," or plays, that were written by someone else.) Jagger and Richards were not setting the world on fire with their songwriting, and the album contained only three original compositions. But by March 1965 England's number one album, EP (extended play record), and single were *all* Rolling Stones records. The Beatles and the Stones began to warily compete with each other to pick the best time to release new material.

While their album was climbing the charts, the Stones continued to tour. One of the more notable dangers of their primitive sound system occurred during a sound check in Denmark.

Two microphones that Jagger was holding made contact and produced a 220-volt arc. The force threw him into Jones, who then
smashed into Wyman, who was knocked unconscious. Wyman
recovered and the Scandinavian tour progressed as planned.

"Satisfaction"

In April the Rolling Stones began their third American tour. On
the night of May 9, 1965, Richards woke up in a hotel room in
Clearwater, Florida, with a guitar riff running through his mind.
Later he described to Victor Bockris how he had recorded the
melody on a cassette tape.

> I dreamt this riff. That was the first time it had happened to
> me. I just woke up, picked up the guitar, and . . . "I can't
> get no . . . satisfaction. . . ." It was pretty funny 'cause that
> night I was so tired. . . . On the tape you can hear me drop
> the pick and the rest of the tape is me snoring.[25]

Within a week the Stones had recorded "Satisfaction" at RCA
studios in Hollywood. Robert Palmer records Jagger's initial
impressions:

> According to Mick, "it sounded like a folk song when we
> first started," a protest song influenced by Bob Dylan.
> By the time the Stones were through, Keith's fuzz-tone
> guitar riff, the charging Memphis rhythm and Mick's
> teasing, deliberately difficult-to-make-out vocals were its
> distinguishing features. In the U.S., the single jumped
> from Number Sixty-Four to Number Four in just two
> weeks, and shortly after that, it became the Stones' first
> American Number One. It repeated this success when it
> was released in England at the end of August, and it sub-
> sequently topped the charts around the world.[26]

Millions of teenagers identified with the frustration, impa-
tience, and veiled sexuality in "Satisfaction." Richards, however, did not like the song. He later said "If I'd had my way,
'Satisfaction' would never have been released. The song was as
basic as the hills and I thought the fuzz guitar was a bit of a gim-
mick. So when they said they wanted it as a single, I . . . said

'NO WAY!' " [27] Keith was out-voted by the rest of the band and the song was released. When the song was included on the Stones album *Out of Our Heads,* that album became the Stones' first number one album in America.

Out of Our Heads began the golden age of Jagger/Richards songwriting. It included such classic songs as "Get Off of My Cloud," "Play with Fire," and "Blue Turns to Grey."

The hit single and hit album were a watershed for the band. In 1965 the Rolling Stones sold 10 million singles, 5 million LPs, and earned more than $5 million on the concert circuit. They went from being a relatively unknown group to a band whose music never stopped playing on the planet 24 hours a day, 365 days a year. Nineteen-sixty-five had them completing two American tours, two European tours, two British tours, and one tour of Australia and Asia.

The money and fame were great, but Keith Richards chose to stay true to the music, as he explains to his biographer:

> "Looking at it over the years, I suppose that the Rolling Stones somehow reverberated to some currently universal vibrational mode. Music has always seemed streaks ahead of any other art form or any form of social expression. After air, food, water, and [sex], I think maybe music is the next human necessity . . . because it's the one thing that will maybe bring you up and give you just that little bit extra to keep on going." [28]

As "Satisfaction" climbed to the top of the charts, the Rolling Stones found out just how brutal the rock and roll business could be. Victor Bockris provides an example:

> "After 'Satisfaction' we all thought 'Wow, lucky us. Now for a good rest,'" Keith said. "And then in comes [manager] Andrew Oldham saying, 'Right, where's the next one?' Every eight weeks, you had to come up with a red-hot song that said it all in about two minutes, thirty seconds." [29]

The Stones were still young and relatively inexperienced. Their tours were generating huge sums of money, but all sorts of parasites and freeloaders were attaching themselves to the band. Between 1963 and 1965, the Stones sold records and concert tickets worth millions of dollars, but little of it made its way into the bank accounts of the musicians. At the time that his music was selling around the world, Richards was paid only fifty pounds a week. When the band returned from tours, they had barely enough money to live. Like their heroes Muddy Waters and Little Richard, they were being ripped off for millions—robbed blind by promoters and handlers.

On Jagger's twenty-second birthday, July 26, 1965, the band signed on with manager Allen Klein, an American. Klein promised the young men that they would be millionaires within a year.

The Shift of Power

With a hit single and a new manager, the Stones were ready to take the world by storm. The social and political scene in which they played a major part was also changing as rapidly as the band.

The success of "Satisfaction" brought down the curtain on the first part of the Rolling Stones' career. Although it had been only eighteen months since they had taken off on their first headlining tour of England, the Stones were now a different band. Robert Palmer sets the scene for the next phase:

> Perhaps the most important change had been the emergence of Mick and Keith as the Stones' songwriters and de facto musical directors, and with it Brian's inevitable fall from grace. Onstage, Brian had always competed with Mick for the fans' attention. He would stop playing his guitar in the middle of a song, begin bashing a tambourine and suddenly lunge toward the lip of the stage, an evil smile illuminating his impish countenance and the alarmingly dark circles under his eyes, his mane of blond hair tossing violently from side to side. Mick was a fluid, sexy dancer, and with Brian vying for the spotlight as well as leadership of the band, he drove himself relentlessly. . . .
>
> With his prominent red lips and almost girlish figure, Mick was attracting male as well as female groupies. He also appealed to straight young men who didn't want to admit he was sexy. . . . A few blues singers had exploited

a certain sexual ambiguity, and it's common among voodoo doctors and shaman types in general. But it was something new in American show business, and if it sold records, the Stones were willing to go along with it. . . . In packaging the Stones, Oldham did more than simply emphasize unisex. He'd set out to make them the group parents would love to hate, the group that was evil and threatening rather than cute, like the Beatles.[30]

As the band toured and recorded relentlessly, Jones always complained to girlfriends that the others were about to fire him. He began to drink heavily, often alone and in secret. He also found a new drug—LSD. Jones began consuming acid as recklessly as alcohol, and it fueled his paranoia. "Brian was the kind of person who would take anything you gave him," recalled one friend. "Offer him a handful of pills, uppers and downers, acid, whatever, and he'd just swallow them all."[31]

After the release of *Out of Our Heads,* the Stones no longer had to depend on American blues and soul covers for material. It seemed the Jagger/Richards songwriting team could do no

The Stones exploited Mick Jagger's sexy dancing style and androgynous appearance to woo both female and male fans.

wrong. The group put out a chart-topping one-two punch in early 1966 with "19th Nervous Breakdown" in February and "Paint It Black" in May. Palmer provides some background:

> [In their songs,] Mick and Keith began to create a world of their own, a world peopled by corrupt debutantes, addled drug abusers in the grip of terminal depression, and average Joes like the narrator of "Get Off of My Cloud," who can't seem to get away from the hard-sell commercials, the nagging telephone calls, complaining neighbors and the other intrusions into personal space that seem inextricably bound up in the texture of modern life.[32]

Like the Beatles, the Rolling Stones had been heavily influenced by the political and poetic song lyrics of Bob Dylan. This influence made the band more aware of the social and political dimensions of pop stardom. Suddenly, the band was taken more seriously as revolutionaries by anti–Vietnam War protesters and other activists at the time.

Between the Buttons

The album *Aftermath* was recorded in 1966, and it was the first Rolling Stones album to consist entirely of Jagger/Richards compositions. The English version of the album contained the eleven-minute song "Goin' Home," which was currently the longest album track in rock history. The album shows the Stones at a halfway point—part blues and soul, part sixties rock. Although Jagger and Richards wrote the songs, Jones's work on the dulcimer, sitar, marimba, harmonica, and other instruments gives the album its organic rock sound.

When the Stones returned to America for their 1966 tour, the country had changed dramatically. Where they had previously encountered men with crew cuts drinking beer, they now found long-haired men smoking marijuana. In addition, LSD was flooding onto college campuses and bohemian neighborhoods.

During the 1966 tour, Jagger would refine his stage act with the help of American soul act, Ike and Tina Turner and the Ikettes, who had been warming up for the band in England. Tina Turner later commented on Mick Jagger:

Have You Seen Your Mother?

American hippies were exhibiting some strange behavior in 1966, but the Rolling Stones went to even wilder extremes. In September they all appeared dressed in women's clothes to film a promotional video for "Have You Seen Your Mother Baby, Standing in the Shadows?" When the single was released a few weeks later, the record sleeve pictured the band standing on New York's Park Avenue, again in drag. Author Philip Norman describes the scene in *Symphony for the Devil:*

> The Stones were photographed as a group of aging transvestites, each one adopting a drag role to which his character seemed only too well suited. Brian Jones ("Flossie") pouted smoke rings in a WAF [British Women in the Air Force] uniform and peroxide wig. Keith ("Molly") in befrogged "costume" and cameo brooch, looked like an archdeacon's wife turned to drink. Jagger, his lips reddened to the size of chipolata sausages, wore a dog-eared tea-dance hat, next to Charlie ("Millicent"), grimly hatted and furred. The centerpiece was a wheelchair in which Bill Wyman ("Sarah") sat, a sullen WAC [British Women's Army Corps], with skinny spinster legs almost tied in a knot.

Two days later, the Stones appeared on Ed Sullivan's show. Jagger minced and flounced across the stage, leering at the camera. Jones was festooned in lace, looking gaunt and haunted, as he attacked his dulcimer with maniacal abandon. Sullivan was appalled and vowed to never let the Stones back on his show. (He later had to eat his words, as the Stones became much too popular to ignore—they appeared on the show several more times.)

While we were out on tour, Mick wanted to learn a dance like I did with my backup group, the pony. I knew he had been watching us every night from the wings. He tried, and I said, "Look at the rhythm on this guy! God, Mick, come on!" I mean we laughed because Mick was serious—he wanted to get it. He didn't care about us laughing at him. And finally he got it, in his own kind of way.[33]

The bold moves of Jagger and the band thrilled hard-core Stones fans. Radio programmers, however, were starting to hear protests about the Rolling Stones from concerned parents and religious and civic leaders. When the Stones released "Let's Spend the Night Together" in early 1967, several American radio stations refused to play it because of its references to sex.

Mick Jagger's bold and sexually suggestive moves on stage excited audiences but drew criticism and protest from many parents and conservative leaders.

When the band appeared on the *Ed Sullivan Show* to promote the single, they gave in to network pressure and agreed to change the words to "Let's spend *some time* together." (Actually, Jagger just mumbled a few phrases to get past the offending idea.)

Days later the Stones released the album *Between the Buttons.* The arrangements were varied and resourceful thanks to Jones's additions of stringed instruments as well as flutes, recorders, and other wind instruments.

Critics loved the album, but storm clouds were gathering over the Rolling Stones. The nonstop touring and continual partying were beginning to take their toll. Brian Jones was teetering on the edge of madness from drug use. Jagger was on the verge of a nervous breakdown. And Richards was starting to use huge quantities of LSD. As press agent Tony Browne says: "You'd bump into [Richards and Jones] and they'd be under the influence of everything. And they looked like they were sixty. . . . They were old men in their twenties." [34]

The Stones Get Busted

Richards had used some of his new wealth to buy a Tudor-style house, complete with a thatched roof, on a country estate called Redlands in Sussex, about ninety minutes south of London. The house had a five-acre lawn and was surrounded by an eight-hundred-year-old moat. The peace that Richards found at Redlands, however, would quickly be shattered by London's tabloid press.

In January 1967 a reporter for the tawdry London paper *News of the World* portrayed the relatively sober Mick Jagger as participating in "LSD orgies." At that point, Jagger had never taken the drug. The reporter was actually talking to a stoned, outspoken Brian Jones in a London nightclub. The reporter mistakenly

Anita Pallenberg

Brian's drift toward self-destruction was temporarily slowed by the arrival of an exotic, worldly German model named Anita Pallenberg. According to Victoria Balfour in *Rock Wives,*

> Anita's long and notorious association with the Stones began in 1965 when she managed to finagle her way backstage at one of their concerts in Munich. Right then and there, Brian Jones took a fancy to her and soon they were rendezvousing for romantic weekends all over Europe. When . . . Brian . . . brought Anita to England to live with him, the arrival of this long-legged, multilingual Italian-born German beauty . . . elevated Brian's status with the others. . . . Anita and Brian, with their identical bleach-blond Beatle-style bobs, were a mischievous pair. . . . But there was a dark side to Brian: He had a tendency to beat up his women. Eventually Anita grew tired of Brian's abusive ways and in 1967 fled into the sympathetic and willing arms of Keith Richards. That union—which lasted a dozen years or so—produced [two children] Marlon . . . and Dandelion Angela.

Following an abusive relationship with Brian Jones, German model Anita Pallenberg began a long-term relationship with Keith Richards. The couple is shown here in a 1971 photo with their two children.

thought Jones was Mick Jagger. When the article appeared, it attracted the attention of the police, who began to follow the band and tap their phones. An angry Jagger announced on a TV talk show that he was going to sue *News of the World* for libel. Jagger's statement drew the wrath of the British press establishment. In the meantime, Richards and Jones were trying to get Jagger to take LSD before they began recording their new album. A party was arranged at Redlands for Saturday, February 12.

On that Saturday, Redlands was alive with a Rolling Stones rock and roll party. George Harrison of the Beatles was there along with Mick Jagger, Marianne Faithfull, and several less-famous friends. They were all high on LSD. Apparently one of the partygoers was working undercover for the *News of the World*. His job was to get the Stones arrested for using illegal drugs, thereby undermining Jagger's lawsuit and exposing the scandalous use of drugs among rock stars. As night fell, the police arrived. They tore apart Richards's home looking for drugs. Four amphetamine pills were found in Jagger's jacket (legally purchased in Italy). Art dealer Robert Fraser, who was a heroin addict, was found to be in possession of twenty-four heroin pills. The police confiscated some marijuana and informed Richards that he would face charges for all the drugs found on his property, even if they belonged to others.

Three months later—on the very day Richards and Jagger were arraigned in court—police raided Jones's apartment in London. They found small amounts of marijuana, cocaine, and amphetamines. As with the Redlands raid, the media had a field day trumpeting the charges against the Stones. The timing of the bust, however, supported the suspicion that the police had a plan to "get" the Stones.

Jagger's and Richards's trials were set for June 27. They spent their time before the court date in Morocco. They had had enough of the touring grind and felt it was time to enjoy their wealth. They also knew that if they stayed in England the police would be watching them. In North Africa, the band sought out opportunities to hear traditional music. They were particularly taken with the rhythms used to accompany mystical dancers called dervishes.

Following a 1967 drug raid, Mick Jagger and Keith Richards were found guilty of drug possession and sentenced to jail terms of three and six months, respectively. Here, Jagger and Richards leave the courthouse smiling after their drug convictions were revoked, thanks to the thousands of fans who protested their sentences.

On June 27, hundreds of fans gathered outside the courthouse where Jagger and Richards were to go to trial. The Stones arrived with one of the priciest criminal lawyers in England. Jagger was found guilty and taken to jail where, tears streaming down his face, he was processed, fingerprinted, and given a prison uniform. Richards was also found guilty. Upon sentencing, Richards received six months in prison, Jagger three.

Outraged at the sentence, British disc jockeys began playing Rolling Stones songs nonstop. Thousands of protesters descended on British consulates in the United States and Europe. Letters to the editor poured into English newspapers. After spending several days in jail, Jagger and Richards were granted bail. A month later a judge threw out their convictions. The musicians were allowed to remain free. The Redlands incident, however, remained one of the most celebrated drug busts of the sixties.

Richards Takes the Stand

When Jagger and Richards were arrested in February 1967, the police found Marianne Faithfull wearing nothing but a large fur rug. The tabloid papers had a field day with the fact that the "rug woman" was the only female among eight men. Faithfull even became an issue when Richards testified in court. In *Blown Away*, A. E. Hotchner excerpts a portion of the trial transcript in which Richards is questioned by prosecutor Malcolm Morris.

MR. MORRIS: There was, as we know, a young woman sitting on a settee wearing only a rug. Would you agree, in the ordinary course of events, you would expect a young woman to be embarrassed if she had nothing on but a rug in the presence of eight men, two of whom were hangers-on and the third a Moroccan servant?

RICHARDS: Not at all.

MR. MORRIS: You regard that, do you, as quite normal?

RICHARDS: We are not old men. We are not worried about petty morals which are illegitimate.

MR. MORRIS: After she had gone upstairs with a woman police officer, did it come as a great surprise to you that she was prepared to go downstairs again into the drawing room wearing only a rug, where there were about a dozen police officers?

RICHARDS: No, sir. After all she had taken off her dirty clothes she had been wearing all day. The rug she was wearing was big enough to cover three women. The girl did not embarrass easily.

The jury deliberated about an hour and came back with a verdict of guilty.

Meanwhile, Jones was hospitalized following a nervous breakdown. In October he was sentenced to nine months in prison for the drug raid at his apartment the previous May. In December the sentence was set aside, but by then his personality had begun to disintegrate.

Chapter 4

The Rise and Fall of Peace and Love

B<small>Y THE SUMMER</small> of 1967 thousands of teenagers had migrated to San Francisco, where they danced to a new kind of music knocking British pop songs off the charts. The new trend, psychedelic music, was pioneered by bands like the Grateful Dead, Jefferson Airplane, Janis Joplin, and Quicksilver Messenger Service. In the words of Grateful Dead bassist Phil Lesh, "Psychedelic music is music that expands your awareness, your consciousness. It's that simple."[35] Many British groups could not keep up with the times and packed up their guitars for good.

The Beatles released their landmark album *Sgt. Pepper's Lonely Hearts Club Band,* and the Stones felt it was time to indulge in the kaleidoscopic sounds of the day. Like others at the time, Jagger immersed himself in esoteric books such as *The Tibetan Book of the Dead,* along with books about meditation and flying saucers. This cosmic influence would be reflected in the words of the next Stones album.

In the fall of 1967 the band released *Their Satanic Majesties Request,* festooned with a lavish, three-dimensional picture on the sleeve. The band was criticized heavily for using "satanic" in the title, but their intention had been no more diabolic than to spoof the wording of British passports: Her Britannic Majesty's / Secretary of State / Requests and requires / in the Name of Her Majesty / all those whom it may concern / to allow the bearer to pass freely.

The controversial title did not help the band's misguided foray into psychedelic music. While critics considered *Sgt. Pepper* the

Sgt. Pepper's Lonely Hearts Club Band

When the Beatles released *Sgt. Pepper's Lonely Hearts Club Band* on June 2, 1967, they forever changed the way albums were made, sold, and even listened to. *Sgt. Pepper*, which cost an unprecedented (at the time) one hundred thousand dollars to record, was the first rock record to contain all the song lyrics on the back of the album cover. The cover featured a lavish photograph of the Beatles surrounded by a crowd of photo cutouts that included Edgar Allan Poe, Bob Dylan, Marilyn Monroe, Karl Marx, and over sixty other personalities. A floral arrangement spelled out the word *BEATLES*. The band members wore satin band uniforms from the 1920s, and sported an entirely new look with feathered hairdos and mustaches.

But *Sgt. Pepper* was much more. It was the first "concept album" in which each individual song was like a chapter in a novel. The theme was that the Beatles were Sgt. Pepper's Lonely Hearts Club Band and listeners were invited to the show. The songs were a crazy quilt of musical styles including rock and roll, folk, vaudeville, Indian, classical, and electronic noise. The album was masterfully blended into a seamless narrative by producer George Martin using two 4-track tape recorders (bands today use up to 128 tracks).

Critical praise for *Sgt. Pepper* was close to unanimous. It was the first rock album to be considered a work of art. After it was released, thousands of bands tried to imitate the album's look and sound because it was believed, at the time, to be the best record album ever made.

Beatles' best work, *Satanic Majesties* was dubbed a catastrophe. As Bill Wyman writes,

> Most critics branded the album a sad, ill-conceived, "druggy" attempt to reply to the Beatles' *Sgt. Pepper*— and John Lennon was among those who disliked it. . . . Rock writer Jon Landau said that *Satanic Majesties* "despite moments of unquestionable brilliance, puts the status of the Stones in jeopardy."[36]

For the first time, Jagger was forced to defend a Stones album: "It's still just an album, not a landmark, or a milestone or anything pretentious like that. All we tried to do is make an album we like with some sounds that haven't been done before."[37]

The poor reception of *Satanic Majesties* brought the Stones to a decisive crossroads in their music. They were unsure which direction to turn. Jagger and Richards still loved African American blues, R&B, and soul music. Jones—after returning from a Moroccan vacation—wanted to revamp the music. He envisioned a unique blend of Moroccan "trance rhythms," Arabic prayer-call melodies, blues, and gospel. Unfortunately, Jones quickly fell back into the partying life in London and never realized his innovative musical dreams.

Beggars Banquet

The year 1968 was a watershed in world politics. A bloody war raged in Vietnam. Protesting young people fell into violent clashes with police. From Berkeley to London to Paris, demonstrators shouted slogans, threw rocks, smashed windows, and stormed police barricades. Both Martin Luther King Jr. and Senator Robert F. Kennedy were assassinated. King's death led to riots in dozens of cities across America. The summer of love had definitely come to an end.

Jagger seized the moment. When protesters stormed the U.S. embassy in London, the singer was driven to the event in his Bentley, jumped out, and mingled with the rioters. He linked

Rowdy antiwar demonstrators at UC Berkeley are pushed back by police. Scenes such as this in the late sixties signaled an end to the era of peace and love.

arms with the protesters for photographs before climbing back into his limousine. When he got home, he scribbled down the words to "Street Fighting Man." When the single was released in August, tensions in America were running high because of violent street protests in Chicago at the Democratic National Convention. Many radio stations refused to play "Street Fighting Man."

Over the summer the band recorded a new batch of Jagger/Richards compositions, including "Jumpin' Jack Flash," "Midnight Rambler," and "Sympathy for the Devil." The songs were hot, and Jones managed to come out of his stupor long enough to contribute some ravishing slide-guitar work. But Jones's sanity would not last. In the early morning hours of May 21, police once again raided his apartment. They found drugs stuffed in the back of his bureau drawer and arrested him.

When the album *Beggars Banquet* was released in December, it was hailed as the band's best album ever. New "underground" magazines on the market such as *Crawdaddy* and *Rolling Stone* trumpeted the album as the Rolling Stones' comeback.

When some critics heard "Sympathy for the Devil" and remembered *Their Satanic Majesties Request,* they were sure the Stones were in league with the devil. Although the song is a powerful political statement—rather than a declaration of religious belief—the Stones' image of "evil" had some basis in truth. As Robert Palmer writes,

> Keith and Anita Pallenberg were dabbling in magical rituals and witchcraft. And everywhere Mick—and especially Keith and Anita—turned, there were drugs, drugs, drugs. . . . Mick and Keith were a dangerous and potentially deadly influence, and too wrapped up in their own interior processes to really notice. There were burn-outs around them, and deaths from drug over-doses, and yet they themselves seemed to emerge unscathed. *Were* they the Devil in disguise? And if so did they deserve any sympathy?[38]

Despite some misgivings about satanism, *Beggars Banquet* delighted most older Stones fans who were glad to see the band

Rock and Roll Circus

While *Beggars Banquet* climbed the charts, the Stones began work on a BBC television special that was intended as a gift to fans who had not seen them perform live for nearly two years. Christopher Andersen writes about the show in *Jagger Unauthorized*.

> Filmed over a three-day period before an audience of eight hundred invited guests . . . the *Rolling Stones Rock and Roll Circus* featured all the standard circus fare—jugglers, animal acts, clowns, and acrobats—as well as Brian in wizard's robes, Charlie Watts in a military uniform and top hat with silver satyr horns, Bill Wyman in ruffled finery, and Keith wearing a drum major's brass buttons and epaulets. Since Jagger was calling the shots, he literally cracked the whip as a crimson-jacketed ringmaster.
>
> While fire-eaters belched flame and trapeze artists swung overhead a roster of megastars appeared in a variety of wild getups: John [Lennon] and Yoko [Ono] were there, he in a harlequin's outfit, she wearing a peaked witch's cap and cape. . . .
>
> There were performances by Lennon, Clapton, and the Who . . . but the highlight of the *Rock and Roll Circus* was the Stones' rendition of "Sympathy for the Devil.". . .
>
> When he [later] screened the program, Mick was struck by how old and tired he looked. . . . Despite the enormous cost Jagger nixed the project. The . . . *Rock and Roll Circus* [was] never . . . seen on the BBC, or anywhere (until it was released in 1997 on video).

getting back to their roots. Today, critics consider the record to be among the band's finest works.

The Death of Brian Jones

In May 1969 Jagger and Marianne Faithfull, who were now a couple, were arrested for possession of hashish. Jones was taking so many drugs and drinking so much alcohol that the other band members gave up on him. In early June, Jagger, Richards, and Watts visited Jones and told him that the band was about to go on tour—without him. Instead of firing their old friend outright, they did what executives of other large companies do in such circumstances: They "accepted" Jones's resignation and offered him a stipend of one hundred thousand pounds a year for the rest of his life. Then, according to Robert Palmer, "they left him to the wolves—the spongers and hangers-on who seemed to always surround Brian and were now staying with him for days on end at his country home, taking his drugs and drinking his liquor." [39]

On July 3, 1969, a month after his departure from the band was announced, Jones was found dead in his swimming pool. The official cause was accidental drowning associated with the consumption of alcohol and barbiturates.

The Stones had already planned a free concert in London's Hyde Park for July 5 to introduce their new guitar player, Mick Taylor. Instead, the concert turned into a wake for Brian Jones. More than three hundred thousand people turned out for the show. Two thousand butterflies were released from the stage. Jagger, wearing heavy makeup and dressed in a filmy white thigh-length tunic, flared pants, a leather choker, and a crucifix, read from Shelley's "Adonais" ("He hath awakened from the dream of life").

The 1969 funeral of Stones' guitarist Brian Jones. Jones's drug-related death came just a month after the band fired him because of his out-of-control drug and alcohol abuse.

Then, as always, it was on with the show. Mick Taylor proved to be a guitar virtuoso whose lyrical lead lines and solos poured from his amp. But the other musicians were not in great shape, and the concert was not one of the band's best.

The Stones quickly bounced back from Jones's death—too quickly for some, who imagined all sorts of sinister conspiracies. By 1969 the Stones were such a huge part of people's fantasies that some believed Jones had been murdered by the band, the Mafia, or supernatural forces.

The day after Jones's funeral, Decca released a new single with two instant classics—"Honky Tonk Woman," and "You Can't Always Get What You Want"—the second song featuring a sixty-voice boys' choir. Before the month was out, the record was number one across the globe.

The 1969 North American Tour

In August 1969 the Woodstock Music Festival was held in a rain-soaked farmer's field near Bethel, New York. More than three hundred thousand people gathered for three days of peace, love, and music, listening to performers such as Jimi Hendrix; the Who; Janis Joplin; Jefferson Airplane; Crosby, Stills, Nash, and Young; Sly and the Family Stone; and others. Despite days of rain, there were no fights or riots at the concert site, no one died, and three babies were born. Woodstock was front page news around the world, and it was said to prove that young people could work and live together in peace.

On October 7, the Stones kicked off their first North American tour in three years. At a press conference before the shows, reporters grilled the band about money. There was quite a bit of grumbling that tickets to the show cost $7.50, an unheard-of amount for a rock concert at the time. The Stones decided they would do a free concert at the end of the tour to thank Americans for their support.

When the tour began the Rolling Stones looked and sounded like conquering heroes—the undisputed kings of rock and roll. Every night the band was introduced with: "Ladies and gentlemen—the Greatest Rock and Roll Band in the World—

The Stones perform at New York's Madison Square Garden during their 1969 North American tour. Despite praise from critics and fans alike, during the tour there was a great deal of negativity among band and crew members, fueled largely by Jagger's and Richards's growing interest in black magic.

The Rolling Stones."[40] The album *Let It Bleed* arrived in record stores just before the New York City concert on November 27.

For the first time in three years, the Stones were back on the road. To outsiders, the four-week tour was as close to perfect as a rock and roll tour could be. But to tour insiders, such as Mick's costume designer, Ossie Clark, negativity abounded. Clark later told writer A. E. Hotchner that

> there was a negative charge in the atmosphere. . . . They had been getting deeper and deeper into black magic. Led by Anita Pallenberg, Keith and Mick had developed a kind of Satanic identification, as if they were openly dealing with the devil. I suppose it was all bound up with the music they were doing, Satanic songs like . . . "Sympathy for the Devil," but it didn't make it less frightening.[41]

A Free Concert at Altamont

According to Clark, Mick's dabbling in black magic intensified as the tour progressed. In December the Stones had planned to surprise Northern Californians with a free concert in San Francisco's Golden Gate Park. The band consulted the Grateful Dead, who had played for free at dozens of concerts in the park. The Dead offered to help the British group organize the event, trusting that their own experience of many peaceful concerts could be duplicated by the Stones. But Jagger reneged his plan to do the free concert without advance notice. Instead, he announced on national television that the band was going to play in the park, whereupon the city of San Francisco refused to issue a concert permit.

After Jagger's foolish announcement, millions of teens, hoping for another Woodstock, started flying, driving, and hitchhiking to San Francisco. Under pressure to find a new location for the concert, the band settled on a ramshackle auto racing arena called Altamont, located on a windswept, barren hill near Livermore, California.

On December 6, three hundred thousand fans who had set out expecting to spend the day in San Francisco's idyllic Golden Gate Park found themselves stranded at Altamont without food, water, or facilities of any sort. Before that day, the largest audience ever assembled at Altamont had been sixty-five hundred spectators for a demolition derby. With only twenty-four hours' notice, the band's crew quickly erected a small stage at the raceway. To provide security, the Stones hired a local Hell's Angels motorcycle club for five hundred dollars worth of beer. Unstable and prone to violence under the best conditions, the bikers were not the best choice to control a crowd that was soon dangerously wired on bad acid and cheap wine. Feeling besieged by the aggressive fans, and berserk on a combination of amphetamines, LSD, and beer, the Angels began indiscriminately beating people with sawed-off pool cues, tire irons, and beer bottles.

"A Nice Day in Hell"

During Jefferson Airplane's set, singer Marty Balin tried to interfere with the beating of a black man near the stage. Balin was knocked unconscious by an Angel. The Grateful Dead were supposed to play next but refused to go on—lead guitarist Jerry Garcia famously described the scene as "a nice day in hell."

Three hundred thousand fans, including the man pictured here, descended on Altamont racing arena in Livermore, California, for a free concert featuring the Rolling Stones, the Grateful Dead, and Jefferson Airplane. The hastily planned event turned into a violent, uncontrollable scene that Jerry Garcia later dubbed "a nice day in hell."

The concert was being filmed, and Jagger, who desired stage lighting, would not play until the sun set. As the temperature dropped, fans made bonfires of old tires for warmth. The ambiance was getting extremely ugly. By the time the Stones took the stage, the audience had sat through six hours of poorly amplified, hardly visible acts, interrupted constantly by charging Angels who were nearing hysteria. As the band ripped into "Sympathy for the Devil," they had to stop and then restart because of a melee in front of the stage. Keith Richards's biographer takes up the story:

> "The violence was incredible," remembered Keith. . . . [But he knew] if he tried to reason with a rock and roll crowd they were lost. He strode to the microphone, pointed directly at a Hell's Angel in the crowd who was beating an innocent bystander, and shouted, "Either those cats cool it or we don't play. I mean, there's not that many of 'em." As the next song ground to a halt in the face of furious beatings, he shouted, "Keep it cool! Hey if you don't cool it, you ain't gonna hear no music!"[42]

Jagger had only sung the first line of "Under My Thumb" when a young man named Meredith Hunter was spotted flashing a gun. Instantly six Hell's Angels swooped down on Hunter, stabbing him to death. The band crashed to a halt.

The other bands had evacuated the site while the Stones were playing. Halfway through the Stones' set, a helicopter pilot rushed onto stage, introduced himself to Bill Wyman as "the last pilot," and said that he was going to leave with or without the band. Writer Victor Bockris includes these recollections from Richards and Wyman:

> The other memory is of the getaway: everyone running up this hill to a hovering helicopter. It was like Vietnam.

> Bill Wyman added: It couldn't even lift off, that's how full it was. We piled in there on top of each other and took off going slantways and when we landed we were going sideways and couldn't come to a stop properly because it was too heavy.[43]

Although Woodstock had been staged only four months earlier, Altamont marked the end of the idealism of the sixties. In addition to Meredith Hunter, three other people died at Altamont from accidents and drug overdoses. (And four babies were born there.) The violence and negative energy of that day were captured in the film *Gimme Shelter*, which was released a year later.

The Stones escaped from Altamont shaken but unscathed. In the minds of many, however, the violence and decadence in the Stones' music were forever linked with the events of that day. Altamont was the last straw for rock fans who had been bothered by the violence and antiwoman lyrics contained in some of the Stones' more famous songs. "They would carry with them the images of death, the demonic faces in the crowd, the scene from *Gimme Shelter* when Meredith Hunter goes down under the Angels' attack,"[44] wrote Robert Palmer. The decade of flower power was over, and the seventies were about to begin.

Chapter 5

The Seventies' Superstars

IN 1970, MUSIC fans the world over were saddened by the breakup of the Beatles. With the Beatles gone, few bands could challenge the supremacy of the Rolling Stones as the world's greatest rock and roll band. But rock was a young person's game, and the Stones had been in the spotlight for almost ten years. After years of drug abuse, the self-destruction of several close friends, and the deaths at Altamont, the Stones no longer felt young. (Jagger and Richards were still only twenty-seven years old, however.)

Over the next few years the Stones would be asked repeatedly if the end might be near. Richards chose to ignore the questions. Bill Wyman and Charlie Watts were living lives of wealthy country squires. Wyman dedicated himself to photography and Watts to jazz music. By this time Jagger was not just a singer in a rock and roll band, he was a world-renowned celebrity. His name appeared more often in gossip columns than it did in music magazines.

Mick Jagger in the Movies

As the seventies wore on, Jagger decided his next career choice should be starring in movies. He practically jumped off the screen in the 1970 semidocumentary *Sympathy for the Devil (One Plus One)*, which captured the Stones recording that song. Mick also starred as an Australian Robin Hood character in the film *Ned Kelly*, released in October 1970. And the chilling *Gimme Shelter*, depicting the horrors of Altamont, began showing in the United States in December 1970.

While these films were in the theaters, Jagger filmed *Performance,* a movie based on the hypnotic scribblings of author William Burroughs, who was also the author of the controversial novel *The Naked Lunch.* The aging Burroughs was a survivor of the Beat Generation of writers that included Jack Kerouac and Allen Ginsberg. In *Performance,* Jagger played a drugged-out pop star who trades identities with a small-time gangster. Richards's girlfriend, Anita Pallenberg, played Jagger's girlfriend in the film. In Robert Palmer's opinion, *"Performance* cleverly portrayed what many had pictured as the Stones' world—a scene that was at once alluring, decadent, druggy and reeking of death."[45]

In the seventies Mick Jagger decided to try his hand at acting in movies. He is shown here sporting a beard for his role as an Australian outlaw in Ned Kelly.

Warner Brothers originally refused to release *Performance* because of its drug-related plot, although a company spokesperson cited "Mick Jagger's unintelligible Cockney accent"[46] as the reason for holding the film back. However, a deal was struck whereby the studio agreed to screen the movie as a benefit for Release, an organization that helped persons arrested for drugs.

The reality of the Rolling Stones was slightly different from *Performance.* By 1970 the royalties from the Stones albums since *Aftermath* had made Jagger and Richards—now known as the "Glimmer Twins"—quite wealthy. Unfortunately, by this time Anita Pallenberg was addicted to heroin. After Richards returned from Altamont, he too began using the drug for the first time. Richards recounts his slide into addiction after the tour for biographer Bockris:

It's only periods with nothing to do that got me into heroin. It was more of an adrenaline imbalance. You have to be an athlete out there, but when the tour stops, suddenly your body don't know that there ain't a show the next night. The body is saying, "Where's the adrenaline? What am I gonna do, go leaping out in the street?" It was a very hard readjustment.[47]

Jagger watched from the sidelines as his girlfriend, Marianne Faithfull, also slid into the abyss of heroin addiction. As a result of Faithfull's downfall, combined with the shock of Altamont, Jagger pulled away from his satanic and hard-drug images. He began to attain a base of power in the glamorous world of society, the arts, and among the movers and shakers of the entertainment business.

Money, Moving, and Marriage

After Altamont, the Stones discovered that their manager, Allen Klein, had not been treating them honestly. They hired a new manager, who showed them that, in spite of having generated $200 million in the past seven years, they would be bankrupt if they stayed in England. The reason for the impending disaster lay in the structure of Britain's tax code: Resident citizens who made as much as the Rolling Stones did were taxed to the tune of 90 percent of their income. The advisability of moving seemed clear. Before they left, the band sued Klein for $29 million.

On March 4, 1971, the Stones began their Good-Bye Britain tour and played sold-out concerts across the British Isles. When it was over, Jagger and Richards moved to St. Tropez in the south of France. Wyman followed, but Watts elected to remain in England. The Stones who had rolled out of the country were now legally limited to spend no more than ninety days a year in Britain. With their departure, London quickly fell from grace as the go-go capital of the Western world.

When Jagger moved to France he left behind long-time girlfriend Marianne Faithfull, who had recently attempted suicide. For a time Jagger enjoyed life as a jet-setting rock star and one of the world's most eligible bachelors. Then he gave his fans a shock when he married Nicaraguan aristocrat Bianca Perez

Moreno de Macias on May 12, 1971. Fans did not know that Macias was pregnant with Jagger's child.

The twenty-one-year-old Macias was the ex-wife of actor Michael Caine and a member of the social elite in St. Tropez. Although the wedding was supposedly a secret, the press had dogged Jagger and Macias for months, reporting on his purchase of a wedding ring in Paris and the application for the wedding license the day before the ceremony.

Macias had one condition before their marriage could proceed: that Jagger first take instruction in the Roman Catholic religion, which he did. The wedding was attended by the Stones, the Beatles, and hordes of paparazzi. Richards, who did not approve of the wedding, begged Jagger not to go through with it and ended up drunk and passed out on the floor during the entire reception.

Life on the Riviera

Jagger, Wyman, and Richards had separate villas in St. Tropez, but they spent most of their time at Richards's house, which was called Nellcôte. It was there that they held recording sessions for their next album, *Sticky Fingers*.

Mick Jagger weds Bianca Perez Moreno de Macias, who was already pregnant with their child, in a small church ceremony. The rather sudden wedding shocked fans and angered Keith Richards, who did not approve of the union.

Nellcôte [was] one of the most fabulous palaces in the whole glamourous region, an enormous, white Roman-style villa. . . . No sooner had [Keith] moved his family and entourage . . . into the luxurious mansion than he started turning it into his very own Graceland. Just as Elvis had gathered a gang to party and play within his big white house, Keith set about gathering a gang of good old boys to rival even the Memphis Mafia. . . . Despite his own simple tastes, Keith was not about to spare any expense in throwing the biggest, longest, most lavish party of his life. Between April and November he spent seven thousand dollars a week—one thousand dollars for food, one thousand dollars for alcohol, twenty-five hundred dollars for drugs, and twenty-five hundred dollars for rent.[48]

Between July and October, the band brought in a large truck full of recording equipment and began recording the album in the basement. It was inconvenient for the musicians to go home, so Richards's mansion began to look like his first apartment in London. The floor was littered with empty bottles,

Gram Parsons

While Mick Jagger was on his honeymoon, Keith Richards practically barricaded himself in the recording studio in St. Tropez. During this period, Richards became close friends with Georgia-born country singer Gram Parsons. A former member of the Byrds and a founder of the Flying Burrito Brothers, Parsons was an innovator who popularized country rock music.

Gram Parsons introduced Richards to the sad inflections and expressive fine points of country and honky tonk music. Parsons stayed at Nellcôte for months, playing informal duets with his host. Working with Richards, Parsons made major contributions to Rolling Stones songs such as "Wild Horses," "Country Honk," "Dead Flowers," "Far Away Eyes," and "Sweet Virginia."

Eventually, Parsons returned to Los Angeles where he recorded his masterpiece *Grievous Angel*. The sensitive southern singer died of a heroin overdose in a hotel room in Joshua Tree, California, in 1973 at the age of twenty-seven. Richards was shocked and saddened by his friend's death. He said he was "shattered for ages."

record albums, half-smoked cigarettes, dirty clothes, and guitars. Despite the fact that the band never got along for more
than a few days at a time, the conditions proved to be ideal for
making the next record. As for Bianca Macias, she was appalled
by the whole scene and told Jagger she never wanted to see
Keith Richards again.

Rolling Stones Records

After the 1969 North American tour, the Stones were disgusted
with Decca. In 1963 the record company had cut a side deal
that was still funneling royalties that rightfully belonged to the
Stones to their former manager, Andrew Loog Oldham. In
addition, Decca had invested money that the Stones had made
for the company in devices that aided American bombers in hit-
ting targets in Vietnam. This infuriated Richards, who said,
"How can you check up on the . . . record company when to get
it together in the first place you have to be out on that stage
every night? I'd rather [record for] the Mafia than Decca."[49]

The band terminated their contracts with Decca and Allen
Klein in 1970. They decided to manage themselves and form their
own record company, Rolling Stones Records, to distribute their
releases. They hired Marshall Chess, son of Chess Records founder
Leonard Chess, to serve as company president. For the label's logo,
they chose the famous lapping tongue that is often incorrectly said
to be modeled after Mick Jagger. According to Richards, "It's Kali's
tongue. Kali is a Hindu female goddess. Five arms, a row of heads
around her, a saber in one hand, flames coming out of the other,
she stands there with her tongue out."[50]

The first single on the new label was "Brown Sugar." Once
again the band was criticized, this time for the welter of antifemale
gibes and apparent racial slurs in the song. But the band insisted
that the lyrics follow a slave ship's cargo from the Gold Coast in
Africa to a plantation in the English colonies. Fans supported the
Stones by pointing out that the band had always been a major sup-
porter of black music and black artists. At various times they had
hired blues legend B. B. King, Ike and Tina Turner, and Motown
great Stevie Wonder to open their concerts.

In 1970 the Stones terminated their management and record contracts in order to become their own managers and start their own record company, Rolling Stones Records. Donning a T-shirt featuring the famous logo of their record company, Jagger performs with his band.

As the band gathered together to record their next album, it was once again easier for them to live at Nellcôte. By this time Richards's drug addiction was the most pressing problem confronting the band. Whereas Richards had once been the energetic center of the music, he now spent hours in the bathroom or passed out in a corner. Since Nellcôte was private property, however, arrests were less likely, and the band worked at its own pace, unhampered by studio rules and schedules.

This studio foray yielded *Exile on Main Street*, a double album that captured a tough, defiant rock band at the height of their musical prowess. The rough muddy sound of the album buries Jagger's vocals under the twin slashing guitars of Mick Taylor and Richards while Wyman and Watts hold down the kinetic rhythm. *Exile* was released less than a month before the Stones kicked off their 1972 tour. Critics and fans registered disappointment at the music's blurred edges and indecipherable lyrics.

Black and Blue

On June 3, 1972, the Stones began another North American tour in Vancouver, British Columbia. Rumors that it might be the last Stones tour prompted two thousand ticketless fans to riot outside the coliseum and attempt to crash the gates. More trouble followed on July 17. A bomb allegedly planted by political radicals in Quebec, Canada, blew up a truck containing the band's equipment. Replacement gear was rounded up, and once again, three thousand ticketless fans rioted.

In December, after the tour was over, Bianca Macias's hometown of Managua, Nicaragua, was hit by a devastating earthquake. Jagger and Macias flew into the devastated area with two thousand typhoid inoculations for the victims of the quake. Meanwhile, the French police were ready to arrest Richards and Pallenberg for possession of drugs. The couple abruptly departed from St. Tropez and moved into a villa in Switzerland.

To critics, *Exile on Main Street* seemed flawed when compared to previous albums such as *Beggars Banquet* and *Let It Bleed*. As the seventies progressed, the Stones' music seemed to unravel. Richards grew increasingly preoccupied with his drug habit, and Jagger lived a social whirlwind of seeing other glitterati

The Stones electrify the crowd at Montreal Forum during the band's 1972 North American tour. Three thousand fans who weren't lucky enough to get tickets for the concert rioted outside the Forum, throwing bottles and stones at police.

and being seen with them. Their next three albums—*Goat's Head Soup* (1973), *It's Only Rock and Roll* (1974), and *Black and Blue* (1976)—seemed to blend into a single, rambling work.

By this point it was hard to get all the musicians into the same studio at one time. Jagger and Richards would record batches of songs, add overdubs or guest soloists, and send the tapes to the other musicians to add their parts. Then they would sift through what they had and choose the best eight or ten songs. Some fans believed that the Stones were tired of trying to live up to their former glory and had decided to trash their reputations on purpose. The simple truth was the band was bored. Mick Taylor grew so bored, in fact, that he left the band late in 1974.

In the United States, *Black and Blue* got more attention for its ad campaign than for its music. A giant billboard on Sunset Strip in Hollywood featured a bruised woman in ripped silk underwear with her hands tied above her head. The caption read: "I'm black and blue from the Rolling Stones and I love it."[51] In response a group called Women Against Violence Against Women protested and called on the record company to take down the offensive billboard.

Before the protest could get too far, *Black and Blue* had pretty much fallen off the charts. Rock critic Lester Bangs wrote the album's epitaph:

> There are two things to be said about the new Stones album. . . . One is that they are still perfectly in with the times . . . the other is that the heat's off, because it's all over, they don't really matter anymore or stand for anything. . . . This is the first meaningless Stones album.[52]

Ron Wood Joins the Band

The ad campaign for *Black and Blue* was inspired by the rising musical movement known as punk rock. Punk offered bands like the Stones two options—change or die. But the Stones' rejuvenation had already begun, unwittingly helped by Mick Taylor's resignation. With his jazzman's flair for melodic invention, Taylor was probably the most accomplished guitarist the Stones

Keith Richards Gets a Blood Change

Heroin addiction is a difficult lifestyle for anyone. Even when paying
for the expensive drug is not a problem, the addict often is hard put
to obtain and conceal an uninterrupted supply. For a high-profile rock
star like Keith Richards, it became impossible to pass through customs
with enough heroin to fend off withdrawal symptoms. When the band
began to play a European tour in 1973, Richards decided he had to get
off heroin. Victor Bockris writes about Richards's treatment in *Keith
Richards.*

> [Keith] had discovered that there was a clinic in Switzerland
> that specialized in an expensive but effective and painless
> three-day blood-cleansing cure. . . . In between playing Inns-
> bruck . . . and Bern . . . Keith . . . checked in to get [his] blood
> cleaned. The treatment involved a . . . process in which the
> patient's blood was passed through a pump, where it was
> [passed through] a semipermeable membrane. This allowed
> toxic substances that had built up in the bloodstream . . . to
> diffuse out of the blood. . . .
>
> From this cure sprang the myth that Keith regularly had the
> blood emptied out of his body and replaced with a fresh supply.
> This Draculan notion is one of the few elements that Richards
> has gone to some pains to correct. . . . "It's quite simple really,"
> Keith explained afterwards, trying to downplay the event. "He
> just changed [my] blood little by little so that there was no
> heroin in [my] body after forty-eight hours."

ever had. But he was never a real rock and roller or a showman,
and many fans felt that he did not quite fit in with the band.

The Stones tried out several lead guitar soloists for Taylor's
spot. When they hit the road for their 1975 tour, Keith's friend
Ron "Woody" Wood was on stage with the band. Although
Woody was younger than the rest of the band, he had known
them since the early sixties, when he was a precocious kid hanging around with Alex Korner at the Crawdaddy Club. In 1975
he was still a member of Rod Stewart's band the Faces. Stewart
was enjoying a solo career and was thinking of leaving the
Faces. Richards offered Woody a permanent gig with the
Rolling Stones. One of the factors the Stones considered when
choosing Woody was "his physical and mental stamina to with-
stand the grueling lifestyle of the road—like a Rolling Stone."[53]

Enter Punk Rock

By 1976 or so, rock and roll was considered dead by many. The revolutionary days of the sixties were long gone. There was a worldwide recession and an energy crisis. And the Stones seemed to be turning into a parody of themselves. But in a few sweaty nightclubs in London and New York, something was happening. Teenagers were fed up with corporate rock played by decadent millionaires. According to Robert Palmer, in *The Rolling Stones,*

Suddenly kids in their teens and early twenties were making their own rock & roll, and if it was rough and crude and abrasive, it could also be deliriously exciting. Almost overnight, it seemed, the music press was full of interviews with performers who called themselves Johnny Rotten, Cheetah Chrome and Poly Styrene and called the Stones and the other Sixties holdouts rich, boring [and] old. . . . Joe Strummer of the Clash . . . made up a singalong for punk audiences that went "no more Beatles, Stones or Who in 1977." It was a kiss off and a challenge.

Featuring such crude artists as Johnny Rotten (above), punk rock music became popular in the late seventies among young people.

Ron Wood was the opposite of Mick Taylor. Sloppy and ragged, he was anything but slick. But he was adept at ripping out biting leads and "slash and burn rhythm."[54] Woody brought to the band energy, high spirits, and a perpetual cockeyed grin—things the Stones had been lacking for a long time.

To kick off the tour on May 1, the Stones tied up traffic in Manhattan by driving down Fifth Avenue playing "Brown Sugar" from the back of a flatbed truck. The end of the tour came in Buffalo, New York, on August 6, where fans rioted, injuring six hundred. The Stones canceled all of their Latin American dates, but they nevertheless returned home $13 million richer.

The Stones were having a good time on stage again; before a year was up, they decided to record a live album. To prepare, the band decided to work some small theaters and nightclubs.

Keith Richards's Canadian Bust

By February 1977, the Stones were on the upswing—except for Richards. When he passed through customs at a Toronto airport, he was so high on drugs that he thought the people looking through Pallenberg's twenty-eight pieces of luggage were Stones employees. In fact, the searchers were members of the Royal Canadian Mounted Police (the Mounties), and they found ten grams of hashish and drug paraphernalia that Richards had used on the airplane. Richards and Pallenberg were allowed to leave while the evidence was sent to be analyzed.

The police kept a close eye on the couple after the airport fiasco. On February 27 a small army of Mounties stormed into Richards's room at the Harbour Castle Hotel, found one ounce of recently purchased high-quality heroin, and arrested the guitarist for possession. The amount was large enough to put Richards at risk for a sentence of seven years to life in prison.

Richards's extensive criminal record did not bode well for him. He had a recent cocaine bust in England; a fine in France for possession of hashish, cocaine, and heroin; and various other offenses going back ten years. And no one could recall anyone escaping such a serious charge in Canada. Meanwhile, after the Mounties had confiscated his supply of heroin, Richards lay on the floor of his hotel bathroom, gagging and vomiting in the grip of acute heroin withdrawal.

Margaret Trudeau, wife of Canadian prime minister Pierre Trudeau, had become something of a Rolling Stones groupie. The young woman took up residence in the Harbour Castle and partied flagrantly with the band in the halls. This behavior drew even more attention to Richards's situation.

But the show must go on, and Richards pulled himself together for the club dates. Rock author Chet Flippo says Richards looked "hollow-cheeked and unshaven, gaunt, and . . . translucently pale" but the music did not seem to suffer. "And Keith, whose soul had been stained blacker than black many years before by the spirit that anointed the legendary Robert Johnson, glowed with internal combustion that no scientist in the western world would want to identify."[55] The result of that concert tour turned media circus was the sloppy blues and reggae album *Love You Live*.

The Stones' legal team managed to secure permission for Richards to leave Canada and work the 1978 tour of the United States. The album *Some Girls* was released that summer and found the band in an optimistic mood mixing disco, punk, fifties rock, and funk

Jagger and Richards jam together during a 1976 concert. Despite his heavy drug use, Richards somehow managed to perform at all of the band's shows.

styles. Critics hailed it as the best Stones album in years.

Keith returned to Toronto to plead guilty to the possession charge. He had not used heroin for months. To everyone's surprise, the judge let him off with a warning and orders to perform a benefit concert for charity. In April 1979 Richards and Ron Wood performed two concerts benefiting the Canadian National Institute for the Blind.

Although Richards had spent the decade in a haze of drug addiction, by 1978 he realized that he had to choose between music and heroin—and possibly jail or death. Keith's newfound sobriety allowed him to explore fresh musical styles with a wide range of players, including blues legend Muddy Waters, jazz super-bassist Stanley Clarke, Buddy Holly's original Crickets, and the crack reggae rhythm team of Sly Dunbar and Robbie Shakespeare.

The 1980s were dawning, and it looked as if the Stones were going to keep the music alive for a long time coming.

Chapter 6

Rolling into the Record Books

As THE 1980s dawned, the Rolling Stones' place in rock and roll history was secure. In November 1979 Jagger and Macias divorced, and he quickly returned to his life as a social butterfly. Richards, too, had ended his long-term relationship with Anita Pallenberg, which had produced three children (the youngest child died at the age of ten weeks). Before long, Jagger was dating Texas-born model Jerry Hall, and Richards was involved with *Vogue* covergirl Patti Hansen, who helped him recover from his addiction to heroin.

The album *Emotional Rescue* was released in June 1980. With no studio time booked and no tour in the works, the band devoted itself to private interests. Then, on December 8, 1980, ex-Beatle John Lennon was shot dead in front of his apartment building in New York City. The Stones were personally devastated by the news—each one felt they had lost a friend and kindred spirit. Once again the band was reminded of how tenuous life can be even with the security of wealth and fame.

Tours, Awards, and *Undercover*

The Stones had been on a work cycle that scheduled a world tour every three years, and in 1981 it was time to gear up once again for the rigors of the road. In September, before the tour began, the Stones announced that their shows would be underwritten by Jovan, Inc., a perfume manufacturer. This marked the first time any rock band had ever accepted a corporate sponsor.

Mick Jagger is hoisted above the heads of thousands of cheering fans at a 1982 concert. Following their 1981–82 world tour, the Stones received numerous awards, including best band of the year, by critics and readers of Rolling Stone *magazine.*

Four days before the tour, the Stones played a nightclub gig to 275 lucky fans in Worcester, Massachusetts. Another 4,000 people showed up, along with riot police and National Guard helicopters. Instead of fighting the fans, the police threw open the doors of the nightclub and the people in the street chose dancing over rioting.

On September 21, Jagger granted the only face-to-face interview of the entire tour—to a twelve- and a thirteen-year-old girl—in North Brookfield, Massachusetts, who were writing for their school newspaper. Jagger refused interview requests from every other newspaper, magazine, wire service, and TV network. The band did appear on TV, however. The second to last show of the tour in Hampton, Virginia, was broadcast on live pay-per-view television—a first for the band. The tour continued in Europe in 1982 and included the first tour of Great Britain in six years.

On March 4, when *Rolling Stone* magazine announced the winners of its Reader's Awards, the Rolling Stones made a sweep. They received awards for best band of the year; best male vocalist; album of the year (*Tattoo You*); best single ("Start Me Up"); best songwriters (Jagger and Richards); and best instrumentalist (Keith Richards). The magazine's Critics Awards gave similar honors to the Rolling Stones.

Undercover was released in 1983. Once again, the Stones enraged critics with their violent song themes. The album included song titles such as "Tie You Up (the Pain of Love)," "Too Much Blood," "Pretty Beat Up," and "It Must Be Hell." The violent lyrics probably had more to do with the growing hostilities between Jagger and Richards in the recording studio than the world situation. And the tense atmosphere among the musicians did not make for a great album. *Undercover* stalled at number four on the charts. It was the first time since 1969 that a Stones studio album did not debut at number one.

Between 1983 and 1988, the Rolling Stones abandoned their three-year tour cycle to disperse into their own projects. Although fans could not see the Stones live, they could attend the movie *Let's Spend the Night Together*, released in 1983. The film was shot during the 1981 North American tour and included seventeen songs.

Birth and Death

The mid-1980s were a time of marriage, birth, and death for the Rolling Stones. On December 18, 1983, Richards celebrated his fortieth birthday by marrying Patti Hansen. On March 2, 1984, Mick Jagger became a father again when Jerry Hall gave birth to the couple's first child, a daughter. In January 1985 Ron Wood married his girlfriend, Jo Howard. In March a daughter was born to Richards and Hansen, and in August Jagger and Hall had another child, a son.

In the midst of all this happiness, tragedy struck. On January 1, 1984, venerated British bluesman Alex Korner died in London at the age of fifty-five. Then, on September 12, 1985, long-time Stones piano player Ian Stewart was having trouble breathing and made an appointment with his physician. While sitting in the doctor's waiting room, Stu suffered a massive heart attack and died.

Though always out of the limelight, Stu kept the Stones in focus. He was the one person capable of mediating between Jagger and Richards. As Charlie Watts said at the funeral: "Who's going to tell us off now?" The Stones all attended the funeral, Jagger looking shrunken and pale—almost theatrically haggard. The Stones played a private memorial concert for Stu in February. It was their first official collaboration in nearly four years.

Jagger Sings Alone

The distance between band members widened in 1985 when Mick Jagger released his first solo album, *She's the Boss*. The album reached number eight in America, number six in Britain. As Jagger did interviews to promote the album, rumors spread that if *She's the Boss* did well, it might mean the end for the Rolling Stones.

The album was not a stunning success, and the hostilities between Jagger and Richards gained more attention than the album in the rock press. When Jagger recorded *She's the Boss,* he put his solo project ahead of the band. This caused the other four Stones to unite against him. Wood and Watts both talked of resigning. In 1986 each band member received a letter from Jagger stating the singer's refusal to tour. Jagger was planning on touring solo, still singing Rolling Stones songs. Keith, never one for understatement, responded by saying, "If Mick tours without this band, I'll slit his . . . throat." [56]

Jagger gave his perspective on his solo career: "The difficulty in growing up is that you start with this gang of people . . . [that] simply can't last forever. It's very childish to think you can remain in the gang all the time." [57] In another interview he said, "The band members were in such bad shape physically, they couldn't walk across the [street] much less go on the road. I'm not nineteen anymore. The Rolling Stones are not my only interest in life." [58]

"The Stones at a Standoff"

On June 13, 1985, a giant transatlantic benefit concert called Live Aid took place with stages in Philadelphia and London hooked together via satellite. Featured were superstars such as David Bowie, Elvis Costello, Phil Collins (who hopped the supersonic Concorde to play in both cities), Paul McCartney (in his first live appearance in seven years), and Robert Plant and Jimmy Page (in their first reunion since the breakup of Led Zeppelin). The Stones refused to play because Jagger and Richards would not appear on the same stage together.

Jagger decided to appear on stage with Tina Turner, singing "State of Shock," and "It's Only Rock and Roll." At the last minute Richards and Woody backed Bob Dylan, in a less than stellar performance.

Dirty Work was released in 1986. It opened with two songs that continued the violent imagery of *Undercover.* The lyrics alluded to flesh, blood, pulp, bruises, holes, and splatter. The song "One Hit" was turned into a video which featured Richards in an all-too-convincing lunge and karate chop at Jagger.

Dirty Work vanished off the charts within ten weeks. The proposed 1986 summer tour was canceled, and other group projects quietly abandoned. The newspaper *USA Today* ran a three-part report on the group titled "The Stones at a Standoff." It detailed the creative, personal, and professional differences in the band.

Meanwhile, Richards played at two sixtieth-birthday concerts for Chuck Berry in St. Louis. The shows were later featured in a film called *Hail! Hail! Rock 'n' Roll.* Woody showed his paintings at gallery openings and appeared in concerts with Bo Diddley, Ray Charles, and Fats Domino. Watts toured the United States with his thirty-three piece jazz band. And the forty-nine-year-old Wyman made headlines in the British tabloids for his love affair with fifteen-year-old Mandy Smith, whom he married in 1989.

In September 1987 Jagger released his second solo effort, *Primitive Cool.* Although critics thought the album was better than *She's the Boss,* it only sputtered up to number forty-one on the American charts. The album was not well received, but Jagger did complete a successful solo tour of Japan and Australia to support the record.

In 1988 Richards was recording and touring with his own band, the X-Pensive Winos. But the failure of *Primitive Cool* caused Jagger to reach out to his bandmates. He summoned them to the Savoy Hotel in London and expressed sadness at recent hostilities. By the next year, the Stones were geared up and ready to get rolling again.

The Steel Wheels Tour

After almost eight years off the concert circuit, 1989 began in a big way for the Rolling Stones. A new promoter agreed to handle their tour and guaranteed the band an unprecedented $70 million. This was not to be an "oldies tour" but a new production with new material from a new album, *Steel Wheels*.

Before the tour took place, the Rolling Stones were inducted into the Rock and Roll Hall of Fame at the Waldorf-Astoria in New York. Wyman declined to appear and Watts could not attend, but Jagger, Richards, Woody, and Mick Taylor were there. All the current and former Stones were inducted, with a special tribute paid to Brian Jones and Ian Stewart. The traditional closing jam session featured Jagger, Taylor, Richards, and Woody, along with Little Richard, Tina Turner, and others rocking the house.

On August 31, the Stones kicked off their Steel Wheels tour in Philadelphia. The two-hour show was packed with raw energy. Critics agreed that the band showed that they were not a bunch of old men trying to rock and roll, they were still as strong and vital as ever. The stage set was reminiscent of that summer's *Batman* movie, with boilers, girders, trusses, ropes, chutes, flame-throwing pipes, and hoses. The bass, guitar, and drums competed with Jagger's wail through a 550,000-watt sound system. And the band pleased the

During a 1989 Steel Wheels tour concert, Mick Jagger and Ron Wood show the audience that the Rolling Stones are still as strong and vibrant as ever.

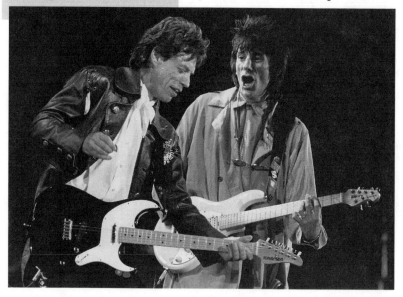

crowd with new material as well as classics such as "Satisfaction," "Paint It Black," and "Midnight Rambler."

The Stones traveled in royal style with private jets, limousines, entire floors of hotels, and security code names. While they had once hosted radical yippies and Black Panthers backstage, now access was afforded to Hollywood stars such as Meryl Streep and Barbra Streisand. On a charitable note, the band donated $500,000 toward relief after the 1989 California earthquake.

The Steel Wheels tour ended in December after the band entered the record books by playing to 3.2 million people at fifty-nine shows and grossing over $310 million. They grossed nearly $12 million in New York alone.

In February 1990, Steel Wheels Part Two took place in Japan. For the first time, Japanese Stones fans were able to see the band live as they played ten sold-out shows in Tokyo. The Stones then rolled on to Europe, where the tour continued with a new stage, new songs, and a new name—the Urban Jungle tour. In July Richards's finger became infected, causing the band to miss three shows—the first time in twenty-eight years that the Stones had missed a show because a band member could not play. Urban Jungle finally ended on August 25, 1990, after forty-six shows in twenty-six cities—almost one year after the start of Steel Wheels.

In October 1991 the Steel Wheels tour was immortalized in a film called *At the MAX*. The film was shot in the IMAX format that could only be shown on a one hundred-foot-wide screen at one-hundred specially equipped IMAX theaters worldwide.

Into the Voodoo Lounge

After Steel Wheels, it was back to family business for the band. Family had become very important to Jagger. He was described in the British press as "a family man, endlessly concerned with his assets, his holdings, his antiques, his gardens, and his wine."[59] In November 1991 Jagger married Jerry Hall. On July 2, 1992, the singer was the first Stone to become a grandfather when Jade, his and Macias's twenty-year-old daughter, gave birth to a daughter.

A scene from the 1991 IMAX film At the Max, *which featured the Stones during their Steel Wheels tour.*

For the next several years, Richards toured exclusively with the X-Pensive Winos, releasing his first solo album, *Main Offender,* in 1992. On January 6, 1993, Bill Wyman appeared on the British TV show *London Tonight,* where he made an official announcement. "I really don't want to do it anymore," [60] said the bass player. He had decided to quit the Rolling Stones after thirty years.

Jagger released his third solo album, the bluesy *Wandering Spirit,* in 1993. At last, one of Jagger's solo albums was a critical success. This blunted the "trauma" of Jagger's fiftieth birthday. It was repeatedly pointed out to him that he was three years older than Bill Clinton, the president of the United States. "But younger," Jagger replied, "than the secretary of state!" [61]

At the end of the year, the band met again to begin recording. The sessions for *Voodoo Lounge* were conducted with Darryl Jones on bass.

On May 3, 1994, the Stones boarded a yacht and sailed down the Hudson River to a pier where the press awaited. With a banner reading *Voodoo Lounge* flapping in the breeze behind them, they announced their coming world tour of 1994–1995.

After their by now-traditional warm-up at a small nightclub, the band kicked off the tour at RFK Stadium in Washington, D.C., on August 1, 1994.

On November 18, 1994, the Stones gave a new meaning to the term "world tour" when they broadcast their Dallas concert over the Internet. At the time, the powerful hardware needed to download the multimedia presentation was not widely available, so the show was received on only two hundred computers worldwide.

The Voodoo Lounge tour continued in 1995 as the band played cities in Central and South America, then South Africa, Japan, New Zealand, and Australia. The tour rolled on through Europe and through the rest of the year.

Low-Tech, High-Tech

While the Stones were on the Voodoo Lounge tour, they found some time to make acoustic recordings of classics such as "Street Fighting Man" and Bob Dylan's "Like a Rolling Stone." These tracks and others made up the album *Stripped,* which was released on November 14, 1995.

After releasing the low-tech acoustic album, the band released the high-tech Voodoo Lounge interactive CD-ROM, which featured a multimedia portion, including video clips of the band, playable on home computers. The CD was released in conjunction with the launching of the Stones' website. The band got more personal on the Internet when Mick Jagger,

Little Boy Blue and the Blue Boys

In 1995 the earliest known recording of Mick Jagger and Keith Richards playing together mysteriously appeared on the auction block at Christie's in London. The thirty-minute reel-to-reel tape was made in 1961 and contained thirteen songs performed by Little Boy Blue and the Blue Boys. It was recorded in a group member's living room—though neither Jagger's nor Richards's. The seller was only identified by Christie's as a former member of Little Boy Blue, now a British senior civil servant. The tape fetched a reported £50,240 (about $81,400). Though Christie's did not reveal the name of the tape's buyer, sources inside the auction company revealed within forty-eight hours that the anonymous buyer was none other than Mick Jagger.

Charlie Watts, and Ron Wood participated in interactive interviews with fans who were able to access the band members via their modems.

Babylon and Beyond

In 1996 a few milestones were added to the Stones' long record. On May 29, 1996, Keith Richards became a grandfather when his son Marlon and supermodel Lucie de la Falaise had a baby girl. In October a newly edited version of the 1968 *Rock and Roll Circus* was released, showing the world a moment frozen in time.

But it seemed the older the Stones got, the harder it was for them to stay off the road. In October 1997 the band kicked off their Bridges to Babylon tour in Chicago. The entourage was serviced by six chefs, including one who made only desserts. In addition, there was a backstage area known as Bar Babylon, where band workers and hangers-on could hang out.

The Chicago show started with an overexcited "Satisfaction." Jagger, at age fifty-four, still shimmied and shook like a twenty-year-old. Richards played with a huge grin on his face, at once childlike and old-man wise. After the show *Rolling Stone* reporter Chris Heath polled the band about the worst part of growing old:

> RONNIE WOOD: When your ankles start to change color [lifts up an ankle and shows off discolored blotches]. . . . I still feel like I'm 23. My kids are, like, "You're so old." That's the hardest thing about old—when the kids rub it in.

> MICK JAGGER: I suppose you think about the time that's allotted to you more than when you were young. The mortality thing obviously has a stronger pull for you. It's an imminent truth.

> KEITH RICHARDS: I haven't found it yet. I still zoom around and do what I do. I'd hate to go 'round thinking about [derisively] health. . . . It's never occurred to me. . . . It's such a sturdy frame, this: I even abused it to see how far it could go, but that was a long time ago. . . . There's only one really fatal disease, I've concluded. It's called hypochondria. And it is deadly.[62]

The Babylon tour saw the release of a new Rolling Stones album, *Bridges to Babylon,* which was hailed by critic John Swenson as the best Stones album in more than twenty years. The album featured an astonishing supporting cast, including jazz saxophone great Wayne Shorter, organist Billy Preston, keyboardist Benmont Tench, percussionist Jim Keltner, and guitarist Waddy Wachtel.

Once again, the Rolling Stones lived up to the title of the world's greatest rock and roll band. Once again millions of fans bought up concert tickets within hours of going on sale. And once again reporters asked the band when they were going to call it quits. Perhaps the

Mick Jagger struts his stuff during a 1997 concert in Chicago, the first stop on the band's Bridges to Babylon tour. The tour was a huge success, with tickets selling out within hours of going on sale.

best answer to that question comes from *Tattoo You* when Jagger sings: "If you start me up, start me up / I'll never stop."

Rocking into the Twenty-First Century

T HE Rolling Stones—and those who knew them intimately—
paid their dues for rock and roll. "There was," one friend rue-
fully pointed out, "really a trail of corpses behind Keith." [63]
Many who tried to keep up with the drug use of the band ended
up dead or ruined—their dreams permanently shattered.

It has been said that Keith Richards has a constitution of
concrete—and indeed he must. But it is impossible to detail the
pain, sickness, and sheer despair experienced by the guitarist—
and those who loved him—as he has repeatedly won and lost
his battles against heroin addiction over the decades. The list of
rock and rollers who died trying to live this destructive lifestyle
reads like a who's who of rock greats: Jimi Hendrix, Janis Joplin,
Jim Morrison, Gram Parsons, Elvis Presley, Sid Vicious, Kurt
Cobain, Jerry Garcia, Shannon Hoon of Blind Melon, and others. The reality is that hard drugs kill. Countless other musicians
have had their creativity, their careers, and their very souls
stolen by their addictions. Keith Richards seems to be one of the
few survivors.

Bridges to the Year 2000

The Rolling Stones have been called everything from the
world's greatest rock and roll band to satanists. The truth probably lies somewhere in between, but one thing can be said of the
Stones: They are survivors, and they have managed to survive
in fine musical form. The Rolling Stones have weathered the
"British Invasion," the psychedelic sixties, the "death of the six-

ties," the disco seventies, the corporate-rock eighties, and remained true to their music into the nineties.

When they hit the stage on their Bridges to Babylon tour, the sound was clear and beautifully balanced. Jagger was singing hard and true and Richards pushed the band into playing its best. Nobody in the stadium was sitting down, and the momentum kept building song after song. The Stones rocked as hard as any band ever has, and all the long years on the stage did not seem to weigh on their songs. It was almost as if they had transcended time and space, and the thirty-five years since their first gigs simply melted away.

The Rolling Stones rocked and rolled like an earthquake. The music liberated, inspired, and strengthened the listeners. Their ages and the size of their personal fortunes was irrelevant; all that mattered was the music. Robert Palmer reaches into ancient tradition in an attempt to explain:

> In West Africa, the drummers who preserve the rhythms of the gods and call them down to possess and cleanse the faithful often receive lavish gifts from wealthy patrons and can amass fortunes equal to a king's. And Africans who know music say a drummer can't play the sacred rhythm with real authority and spiritual force until he's at least forty.[64]

On the 1998 Bridges to Babylon tour, Jagger and Richards were both fifty-four years old. If there's a lesson to be learned from the Stones, it's that what you look like, where you come from, and how old you are don't matter. What does matter in the end is being true to yourself. And to the spirit of the music.

Notes

Introduction: Ladies and Gentlemen, the Rolling Stones!
1. Quoted in Bill Wyman, with Ray Coleman, *Stone Alone*. New York: Viking, 1990, p. 90.
2. Quoted in A. E. Hotchner, *Blown Away: The Rolling Stones and the Death of the Sixties*. New York: Simon & Schuster, 1990, p. 51.
3. Quoted in Hotchner, *Blown Away*, p. 52.
4. Quoted in James Karnbach and Carol Bernson, *It's Only Rock 'n' Roll*. New York: Facts On File, 1997, p. 8.
5. Wyman, *Stone Alone*, p. 3.
6. Wyman, *Stone Alone*, p. 3.

Chapter 1: The Early Days
7. A. E. Hotchner, *Blown Away*, p. 42.
8. Quoted in Hotchner, *Blown Away*, p. 50.
9. Quoted in Hotchner, *Blown Away*, p. 49.
10. Quoted in Hotchner, *Blown Away*, p. 50.
11. Victor Bockris, *Keith Richards*. New York: Poseidon Press, 1992, p. 38.
12. Quoted in Hotchner, *Blown Away*, pp. 73–74.
13. Bockris, *Keith Richards*, p. 54.
14. Quoted in Bockris, *Keith Richards*, p. 55.
15. Robert Palmer, *The Rolling Stones*. New York: Doubleday, 1983, p. 36.
16 Palmer, *The Rolling Stones*, p. 36.

Chapter 2: Up and Down in Rock and Roll
17. Quoted in Bockris, *Keith Richards*, p. 58.
18. Quoted in Bockris, *Keith Richards*, p. 57.
19. Wyman, *Stone Alone*, p. 148.
20. Quoted in Bockris, *Keith Richards*, p. 67.
21. Quoted in Palmer, *The Rolling Stones*, p. 68.
22. Palmer, *The Rolling Stones*, p. 73.
23. Quoted in Bockris, *Keith Richards*, p. 79.

Chapter 3: Topping the Charts
24. Hotchner, *Blown Away*, p. 131.
25. Quoted in Bockris, *Keith Richards*, p. 92.
26. Palmer, *The Rolling Stones*, p. 81.
27. Quoted in Bockris, *Keith Richards*, p. 93.

28. Quoted in Bockris, *Keith Richards*, p. 94.
29. Bockris, *Keith Richards*, p. 94.
30. Palmer, *The Rolling Stones*, p. 82.
31. Quoted in Palmer, *The Rolling Stones*, p. 90.
32. Palmer, *The Rolling Stones*, p. 95.
33. Quoted in Christopher Sandford, *Mick Jagger: Primitive Cool*. New York: St. Martin's Press, 1993, p. 95.
34. Quoted in Bockris, *Keith Richards*, p. 120.

Chapter 4: The Rise and Fall of Peace and Love

35. Quoted in Robert Palmer, *Rock and Roll: An Unruly History*. New York: Harmony Books, 1995, p. 157.
36. Wyman, *Stone Alone*, p. 474.
37. Quoted in Wyman, *Stone Alone*, p. 475.
38. Palmer, *The Rolling Stones*, p. 152.
39. Palmer, *The Rolling Stones*, p. 156.
40. Quoted in Bockris, *Keith Richards*, p. 167.
41. Quoted in Hotchner, *Blown Away*, p. 316.
42. Bockris, *Keith Richards*, p. 169.
43. Bockris, *Keith Richards*, p. 170.
44. Palmer, *The Rolling Stones*, p. 183.

Chapter 5: The Seventies' Superstars

45. Palmer, *The Rolling Stones*, p. 191.
46. Quoted in Karnbach and Bernson, *It's Only Rock 'n' Roll*, p. 27.
47. Quoted in Bockris, *Keith Richards*, p. 174.
48. Bockris, *Keith Richards*, p. 188.
49. Quoted in Bockris, *Keith Richards*, p. 176.
50. Quoted in Bockris, *Keith Richards*, p. 178.
51. Bockris, *Keith Richards*, p. 243.
52. Quoted in Bockris, *Keith Richards*, p. 243.
53. Karnbach and Bernson, *It's Only Rock 'n' Roll*, p. 32.
54. Palmer, *The Rolling Stones*, p. 223.
55. Chet Flippo, *On the Road with the Rolling Stones*. New York: Doubleday, 1985, p. 83.

Chapter 6: Rolling into the Record Books

56. Quoted in Christopher Andersen, *Jagger Unauthorized*. New York: Delacorte Press, 1993, p. 378.
57. Quoted in Sandford, *Mick Jagger: Primitive Cool*, p. 265.
58. Quoted in Andersen, *Jagger Unauthorized*, p. 378.
59. Quoted in Sandford, *Mick Jagger: Primitive Cool*, p. 273.
60. Quoted in Karnbach and Bernson, *It's Only Rock 'n' Roll*, p. 48.
61. Quoted in Andersen, *Jagger Unauthorized*, p. 411.
62. Chris Heath, "Notes from the Babylon Bar," *Rolling Stone*, December 11, 1997, p. 48.

Epilogue: Rocking into the Twenty-First Century

63. Quoted in Bockris, *Keith Richards*, p. 390.
64. Palmer, *The Rolling Stones*, p. 250.

Important Dates in the Lives of the Rolling Stones

October 24, 1936
Bill Wyman, the Rolling Stones' bassist, is born William George Perks in London.

July 18, 1939
Ian Stewart, the Stones' keyboard player, is born in the fishing village of Fife, Scotland.

June 2, 1941
Charles "Charlie" Robert Watts, the Stones' drummer, is born in London.

February 28, 1942
Lewis Brian Hopkins-Jones, or Brian Jones, the Stones' first rhythm guitarist, is born in Gloucestershire, England.

July 26, 1943
Michael "Mick" Philip Jagger, lead singer of the Stones, is born in Kent, England.

December 18, 1943
Keith Richards, the Stones' guitarist, is born in Kent, England.

June 1, 1947
Ron Wood, who would become a Stones guitarist in 1975, is born in London.

January 17, 1949
Michael "Mick" Kevin Taylor, who would replace Brian Jones in 1969, is born in Hertfordshire, England.

October 1961
Mick Jagger, carrying an armload of blues records, runs into Keith Richards at the Dartford, Kent, train station. Mick asks Keith to join his band, Little Boy Blue and the Blue Boys.

July 11, 1962
The band plays its first gig as the Rolling Stones, working through a set of R&B songs at the Marquee.

December 15, 1962
Bill Wyman plays his first gig with the Rolling Stones.

January 17, 1963
Charlie Watts plays his first gig with the Stones but keeps his day job as a graphic artist at an advertising agency.

July 13, 1963
The Stones make their TV debut on the pop music program *Thank Your Lucky Stars.*

September 20, 1963
The Rolling Stones begin their first tour of the United Kingdom as a support act for the Everly Brothers and Bo Diddley.

May 2, 1964
The first Stones LP album, simply titled *The Rolling Stones,* is released by Decca Records. The album is soon released in the United States as *The Rolling Stones— England's Newest Hitmakers.*

June 5, 1964
The band begins its first American tour at Swing Auditorium in San Bernardino, California.

October 25, 1964
The Stones play the *Ed Sullivan Show.*

May 9, 1965
Keith Richards wakes up in a Florida hotel room and writes the first few bars of "Satisfaction."

April 15, 1966
The band releases *Aftermath,* the first Rolling Stones album to consist entirely of Jagger/Richards compositions.

December 8, 1967
The band releases the album *Their Satanic Majesties Request.*

December 6, 1968
The album *Beggars Banquet* is released.

June 5, 1969
Brian Jones is fired from the Rolling Stones with the offer of one hundred thousand pounds a year for the rest of his life. On July 3 he is found dead in the swimming pool at his home.

July 5, 1969
The band plays a free concert in London's Hyde Park as a wake for Brian Jones and to introduce their new guitar player, Mick Taylor.

December 5, 1969
The Stones release the album *Let It Bleed.*

December 6, 1969
Three hundred thousand fans descend on a barren speedway in Livermore, California for a free Stones concert. The Hell's Angels are hired for security but end up beating dozens of fans and killing one man.

May 12, 1971
Mick Jagger marries Bianca Perez Moreno de Macias in St. Tropez.

May 14, 1971
The album *Sticky Fingers* is released.

May 12, 1972
The band releases *Exile on Main Street.*

August 31, 1973
The Stones release *Goat's Head Soup.*

October 18, 1974
The band releases *It's Only Rock and Roll.*

November 29, 1974
Mick Taylor quits the band. Ron Wood replaces Taylor on April 14, 1975.

April 20, 1976
The Stones release the album *Black and Blue.*

February 27, 1977
Keith Richards is arrested in Canada for possession of one ounce of heroin.

June 9, 1978
The album *Some Girls* is released.

November 2, 1979
Jagger divorces Macias.

June 24, 1980
Emotional Rescue is released.

December 18, 1983
Richards celebrates his fortieth birthday by marrying girlfriend Patti Hansen.

March 4, 1985
Mick Jagger releases his first solo album, *She's the Boss.*

September 12, 1985
Ian Stewart suffers a massive heart attack and dies.

March 25, 1986
The Stones release *Dirty Work.*

August 31–December 19, 1989
The Steel Wheels tour, which puts the band into the record books for having played to 3.2 million people at fifty-nine shows and grossing over $310 million.

November 21, 1991
Jagger marries Jerry Hall.

July 2, 1992
Jagger is the first Stone to become a grandfather when his twenty-year-old daughter, Jade, gives birth to a baby girl.

January 6, 1993
Bill Wyman quits the Rolling Stones after thirty years.

August 1, 1994
The Stones kick off the Voodoo Lounge tour at RFK Stadium in Washington, D.C.

May 29, 1996
Keith Richards becomes a grandfather.

October 12, 1996
A newly edited version of *Rock 'n' Roll Circus* is released.

October 1997
The band kicks off their Bridges to Babylon tour in Chicago.

For Further Reading

Victor Bockris, *Keith Richards*. New York: Poseidon Press, 1992. This book is of recent vintage and is full of exciting moments and great firsthand quotes from the Stones' guitarist as well as friends and lovers.

A. E. Hotchner, *Blown Away: The Rolling Stones and the Death of the Sixties*. New York: Simon & Schuster, 1990. The author tends to portray the band in an honest, if unflattering, light. Many quotes from people close to the band are included

James Karnbach and Carol Bernson, *It's Only Rock 'n' Roll*. New York: Facts On File, 1997. A comprehensive book that contains a complete Rolling Stones day-by-day chronology, a complete schedule of their tours and concerts, an extensive and detailed study of the Stones' recording sessions, a discography of all the band's singles, EPs, LPs, and bootlegs, and a list of all their TV, video, and movie appearances.

Robert Palmer, *The Rolling Stones*. New York: Doubleday, 1983. A large book full of great photographs of the band along with a well-written, almost poetic text by the late rock writer Robert Palmer.

Bill Wyman, with Ray Coleman, *Stone Alone*. New York: Viking, 1990. The only book by an actual member of the Rolling Stones. Wyman provides a look at the band's workaday tasks. The book ends with the death of Brian Jones in 1969.

Works Consulted

Christopher Andersen, *Jagger Unauthorized*. New York: Delacorte Press, 1993. A gossipy biography of Mick Jagger with a few revelations about the singer's marriages, drug use, and business dealings.

Victoria Balfour, *Rock Wives*. New York: Beech Tree Books, 1986. An insightful book about the hard lives and good times of the wives, girlfriends, and groupies of male rock and roll stars.

Stanley Booth, *Dance with the Devil*. New York: Random House, 1984. This book, written by a young journalist who had the cooperation of the band, offers an insider's account of the Stones' entrée into the big time and is full of the Stones' tour gossip.

Chet Flippo, *On the Road with the Rolling Stones*. New York: Doubleday, 1985. A rock writer's day-to-day diary as he accompanies the band on their infamous 1977 tour when Keith Richards was busted for heroin in Canada.

Philip Norman, *Symphony for the Devil*. New York: Simon & Schuster, 1984. The author delivers a respectful and competent biography. Norman's analysis of the characters in the Rolling Stones is deep and thoughtful.

Robert Palmer, *Rock and Roll: An Unruly History*. New York: Harmony Books, 1995. A companion volume to a PBS television series on rock that aired in 1995. Lavishly illustrated; each chapter features a timeline of notable events.

Christopher Sandford, *Mick Jagger: Primitive Cool*. New York: St. Martin's Press, 1993. A comprehensive biography of the lead singer of the world's greatest band. Contains excerpts from Jagger's FBI files.

Ken Tucker, *Rock of Ages*. New York: Rolling Stone Press, 1986. A book written and published by the people at *Rolling Stone* magazine about the history of rock and roll that includes details of the Rolling Stones.

Index

Picture Credits

About the Author

Stuart A. Kallen is the author of more than 125 nonfiction books for children and young adults. He has written about topics from the 1980s, ranging from Soviet history to rock and roll to the space shuttle. Kallen has been a singer, songwriter, and guitarist since he was seven years old. He first lip-synched "Satisfaction" in the mirror when he was ten. Kallen lives in San Diego, California.